The Dilemmas of Engagement
The role of consultation in governance

The Dilemmas of Engagement
The role of consultation in governance

Jenny Stewart

ANU
THE AUSTRALIAN NATIONAL UNIVERSITY

E PRESS

ANU
E PRESS

the Australia and New Zealand
School of Government

Published by ANU E Press
The Australian National University
Canberra ACT 0200, Australia
Email: anuepress@anu.edu.au
This title is also available online at: http://epress.anu.edu.au/dilemmas_citation.html

National Library of Australia
Cataloguing-in-Publication entry

Author:	Stewart, Jenny, 1950-
Title:	Dilemmas of engagement : the role of consultation in governance / Jenny Stewart.
ISBN:	9781921536823 (pbk.) 9781921536830 (pdf)
Series:	ANZSOG series.
Notes:	Bibliography.
Subjects:	Political planning--Citizen participation.
	Political participation--Australia.
	Policy sciences--Australia.
Dewey Number:	320.6

Cover design by John Butcher

Funding for this monograph series has been provided by the Australia and New
Zealand School of Government Research Program.

John Wanna, *Series Editor*

Professor John Wanna is the Sir John Bunting Chair of Public Administration at the Research School of Social Sciences at The Australian National University. He is the director of research for the Australian and New Zealand School of Government (ANZSOG). He is also a joint appointment with the Department of Politics and Public Policy at Griffith University and a principal researcher with two research centres: the Governance and Public Policy Research Centre and the nationally-funded Key Centre in Ethics, Law, Justice and Governance at Griffith University. Professor Wanna has produced around 20 books including two national text books on policy and public management. He has produced a number of research-based studies on budgeting and financial management including: *Budgetary Management and Control* (1990); *Managing Public Expenditure* (2000), *From Accounting to Accountability* (2001); *Controlling Public Expenditure* (2003); *Yes Premier* (2005); *Westminster Legacies: Democracy and Responsible Government in Asia and the Pacific* (2005); *Westminster Compared* (forthcoming) and most recently *The Reality of Budget Reform in the OECD* (forthcoming). He is completing, with John Butcher and Ben Freyens, a study of service delivery in the Australian government, entitled *Policy in Action* (with UNSW Press). He was a chief investigator in a major Australian Research Council funded study of the Future of Governance in Australia (1999-2001) involving Griffith and the ANU. His research interests include Australian and comparative politics, public expenditure and budgeting, and government-business relations. He also writes on Australian politics in newspapers such as *The Australian*, the *Courier-Mail* and *The Canberra Times* and has been a regular state political commentator on ABC radio and TV.

Table of Contents

Jenny Stewart

Jenny Stewart is Professor of Public Policy in the School of Business, Australian Defence Force Academy. Prior to that, Jenny held the position of Associate Professor in Public Policy in the Faculty of Business and Government at the University of Canberra, where she continues to serve as Adjunct Professor.

Jenny researches, teaches and writes in the fields of policy analysis, change management and public sector reform. Her books include *The lie of the level playing field*, (Text Publishing 1994), *Renegotiating the environment: the power of politics* (co-authored with Grant Jones and published by Federation Press in 2003), *The decline of the tea lady: management for dissidents* (Wakefield Press, 2004) and *Public Policy Values* (Palgrave Macmillan 2009).

Acknowledgments

My grateful thanks to the many people who contributed their experience, ideas and feedback to this monograph.

I would like to mention, in particular, John Butcher and Professor John Wanna of the Australia and New Zealand School of Government (ANZSOG) and all the participants in the Consultative Forum that took place at the University of Canberra in August 2008. Those who contributed case studies are acknowledged in the text. Others should be mentioned here: Marian Sawer, Lyn Carson, Meredith Edwards, Robyn Keast, Tim Reddel, Carolyn Hendriks, Barbara Pamphilon, Deb Foskey, Gary Humphries, Simon Viereck, Jacqui Lavis and Penny Farnsworth.

Thanks to you all.

Jenny Stewart
Canberra
March 2009

Introduction

To what extent should governments seek input from citizens and stakeholders into the processes of policy making and the business of governance? Many public servants express a degree of ambivalence on this question. While consultation with stakeholders has a long history, wider forms of engagement (in which 'outsiders' are potentially directly involved in decision making) are often seen as impractical or risky, or both.

This research monograph seeks to establish a case for proactive engagement (by public managers) of those 'outside' normal policy communities in Australian policy making. I argue that there are theoretical and practical reasons for a more adventurous approach. It is true that there are many potential pitfalls, for both consulters and the consulted, in extending public policy in this way. The research reported here discusses these and also suggests ways of avoiding them.

The discussion is developed along theoretical and practical lines. I have sought to bring out key themes from the large and sprawling academic literature that has grappled with the task of building conceptual tools to understand engagement. In addition, I convened a project of practical research—the 'dilemmas project'—in order to add to the stock of relevant case studies. These case studies, which form the basis of Chapters 4 and 5 of this monograph, were presented and discussed at a special forum at which practitioners (from within government and without) shared their perspectives. Above all, I have tried to relate the existing literature and this developing research to the central (if vexed) question: what works?

'What really works?' is always a vexed question, because it can be answered only in relation to the values, expectations and purposes of those participating in any given system (and/or of those analysing it). While there are technical dimensions to the issues (for example, in relation to designing consultation so that it meets a specified need or objective), the more fundamental questions go the heart of the politics of policy making.

If managers are to maximise the benefits of engagement, they must be prepared to discuss these political questions, rather than hoping engagement itself will somehow smooth them away. This is, perhaps, the fundamental dilemma of engagement: that those seeking its benefits must be prepared to share some of their power with those outside the system. Deciding when, how or indeed whether to do this can be a tough call.

This monograph is not an engagement 'manual'. It will not tell the manager what to do when. Rather, its objective is to provide ways of *thinking through engagement in practical contexts*. The first half of the monograph sets out what is known, in broad terms, about engagement. Rather than simply 'rehearse' the extant literature, I have presented it in relation to the 'sticking points', the dilemmas of engagement.

The discussion then moves on to theoretical questions. It is important to discuss the normative arguments about engagement—that is, should public managers do all they can to encourage engagement because it widens and deepens our democracy? I then consider practical arguments for and against engagement, before moving on to an overview of general trends in Australia and elsewhere. The empirical heart of the book examines engagement in many different sites and settings, drawing out the importance of context and highlighting (from a number of perspectives) the problematic aspects of the process. Finally, these problems are further analysed to bring out the fundamental dilemmas of engagement: dilemmas of risk, control and values.

1. Conceptualising engagement

In the broadest sense, engagement is a form of participation, a way of involving (or sometimes, re-involving) citizens in the processes of governance. A fundamental concept in democratic theory, 'participation' emerged as a concern in the radical 1960s as a reaction against the dominating influence of big business and big government. The term 'participative democracy' describes the theoretical arguments for reinventing democracy in this way (see Pateman 1970). 'Deliberative' or 'discursive' democracy describes the theory and practice of implementing participation by generating direct 'conversations' between government and citizens (compare Dryzek 1990, 2000). Participation is, therefore, a significant value in its own right, one that can (and in my view should) be pursued for its own sake.

'Engagement' is clearly a related concept, but it is more instrumentalist in character. By engagement, I mean deliberate strategies for involving those outside government in the policy process. 'Policy process', in this context, means ways of making policy decisions and ways of implementing them. It encompasses, in particular, the processes of 'horizontal' engagement, through which those in government (the political and bureaucratic executives) relate to those who are not in direct power relations with them.

Engagement concerns the constitutive aspects of policy making—that is, not the authoritative allocations implied by hierarchy, but the more fluid relationships implied by networks (Colebatch 2002). While engagement can develop in its own way, and along its own lines, it is clearly an area in which the values of public servants (and their political masters) are of prime importance in determining the extent to which it occurs and the extent to which policy is altered as a result.

There is a long history, in political science, of attempts to classify or categorise the ways in which policy making intersects with the interests it affects. From a management point of view, however, description must morph into prescription and characterisations into strategies. It is usual to classify these strategies according to the extent to which they 'engage' (in the sense of involve) particular groups of interest (see Table 1.1). These degrees of involvement are often thought of as a continuum, with particular actions or activities corresponding to, or being typical of, that degree of engagement.

Table 1.1 The continuum of engagement

	Type of engagement	Strategy and target
Increasing participation	Information	Informing citizens of proposed policy changes
	Consultation	Seeking feedback/comment from the public (community consultation) and/or from stakeholders
	Deliberation	Fostering formation/transmission of new views/opinions through structured conversations among citizens
	Partnerships	Contracting with non-governmental organisations to perform functions such as service delivery
	Participatory governance	Involving 'outsiders' in policymaking functions
	Delegation	Giving full authority to bodies outside government to make key decisions

While these kinds of distinctions are useful, it is important not to take them too far. Issues of process need to be distinguished from those of context. The Organisation for Economic Cooperation and Development (OECD 2003), for example, distinguishes between 'giving information' (essentially a one-way activity) and 'consultation' (essentially a two-way activity), with 'active participation' constituting a third level. Empirically, however, when we look at the way policies move and evolve, we find that it is almost impossible to analyse what is happening in this clear-cut fashion. Interaction and exchange occur in multiple ways, and are reflective of evolving relationships.

Engagement and power

Because of the importance of relationships, characterisations of engagement should not be regarded as a menu of choices from which managers can pick and choose. It is important to recognise that engagement is shaped by power relationships and by the rules that govern what participants may and may not do. Public managers are not autonomous beings, but must operate in highly political (and often politicised) environments, in which access to the arenas of power is a much-contested resource.

We should remember, too, that those outside government have their own ideas about when, how and to what purpose they wish to be consulted. The boundary between what is inside and what is outside the State is constantly changing. The boundary itself might be becoming increasingly porous. Some commentators argue that information technologies, particularly networking tools and the 'blogosphere', are bypassing conventional policy altogether (Benkler 2006:21–2).

From the manager's point of view—these factors notwithstanding—forms of engagement reflect not only a logic of appropriateness, but a logic of obligation. The logic of appropriateness describes the sense of 'fit' between circumstances and objectives. This logic is, however, shaped by a logic of obligation, which reflects the degree of compulsion or pressure to consult. It is true that public servants have a duty to consult with those who will be affected by policy choices and, increasingly, this duty is spelled out as a component of specific pieces of legislation and also in more generally based consultative policies.

There is, however, also a harder form of Realpolitik lurking beneath these choices. When the choice is government's alone, it can consult with people to any extent it wishes and use (or not use) what they say, depending on the specifics of the situation. When governments consult because they have to (either because the interests concerned are powerful or ministers insist on it), they have passed beyond consultation to forms of negotiated participation in governance.

The history of writing about engagement reflects this tension within the idea of obligation. Arnstein's famous 'ladder' of engagement was, in fact, a highly political paper dating from the more radical era of the 1960s, when citizen participation meant (ideally) 'citizen control'. Citizen control occupied the top rung of the participation ladder. As citizen control was lost, so corporate manipulation increased (Arnstein 1969).

Later developments of the idea 'managerialised' it, so that participation became one aspect of a suite of tools for public managers to use (Bishop and Davis 2002; Catt and Murphy 2003). From this perspective, degrees of engagement became degrees of loss of government control, rather than loss of citizen control. Table 1.1, for example, starts with the simple transfer of information and ends with 'delegated' situations (such as referenda) in which governments are obliged to heed the results. Delegation can also imply situations in which decision making is handed over to the community or to stakeholders.

Whatever we think of these models (and they have been contested in the academic literature), they do at least highlight the fact that engagement raises questions of power or, in the practical sense, issues of control (Edwards 2008). Power shifts downwards and outwards to the extent that interests external to government are able to influence (or shape) policy values and their implementation.

Metaphors of engagement: ladders or stars?

While it has been traditional to regard engagement as a type of 'ladder' or, less metaphorically, as a continuum, contemporary thinking sees engagement in more fluid terms. One possible metaphor is to see engagement as a star-like arrangement of techniques and sites, with each arm of the star corresponding to a particular set of opportunities. From this perspective, types of engagement are strategies corresponding to different kinds of situations and outcomes, rather than indices of power differentials. Note that the definitions that follow are 'types', set up to clarify terrain and possibilities, rather than clearly demarked empirical realities.

Consultation emphasises information exchange. It can be broadly or narrowly based, but its intent is to elicit response, or to gauge reaction, rather than to include or to incorporate. Consultative strategies do not aim to change preferences; their primary intent is to find out what those preferences are. *Deliberation* describes the use of processes for the evolution of citizen preferences. In other words, deliberation is as much a vehicle of learning as it is of representation.

Deliberation can be thought of as having a weak and a strong form. In its weak form, it is used as an indication as to what a representative group of citizens, fully instructed, might resolve on a particular issue. A number of techniques, such as deliberative polls and citizen juries, are used to structure the discussion. In this form, deliberation is best regarded as a form of designed consultation, in which the opinions of citizens are 'mixed' with substantive policy information. In their strong form, deliberative assemblies can carry a powerful weight in their own right.

Partnerships bring 'outsiders' (often in the form of not-for-profit or for-profit agencies) into contractual relationships with government. Partnership-related consultation, therefore, is geared towards implementation (although depending on the scale and type of partnership, it could have major policy implications as well). The terms of this form of engagement are defined by the work to be done and can involve service delivery or co-production of policy resources (such as training programs).

Participatory governance gives stakeholders the opportunity to engage in policy making directly. The result is cross-boundary forms of negotiated order that involve government agencies and other stakeholders in policy formulation and implementation. Again, this is not entirely a new phenomenon (forms of corporatist policy making are partial examples). What are different are the range and depth of stakeholder involvement and the development of networked relationships between bureaucratic players.

Who to engage?

If engagement is a form of participation, a key question, conceptually and practically, is 'Who will participate?' This question can never be answered definitively, but finding good ways of visualising the problem can be helpful. If, following the Canadian political scientist Paul Pross, we regard governance as a series of concentric circles, with the key institutions of cabinet and the coordinating departments in the centre, other agencies close by, organised interests further out and the community further away, we see that answering this question means making choices about how inclusive we (as public managers) want a process to be (Pross 1986). As with any value, inclusivity has its risks (and choices can be constrained by external factors anyway). Setting out the 'who' of engagement in this way does, however, enable us to name some of the key features.

Community

Let us start at the outer ring of the set of notional concentric circles—with 'the community'. Communities are groups with shared values and a sense of interdependence; they are in a sense the underpinning of social capital. (Social capital refers to the stock of goodwill, or trust, that develops from mutual engagement.) Communities need not be geographically defined. They can represent coalitions of citizens with shared commitments and values—for example, the ACT Mental Health Consumers' Network brings together those with a shared experience of living with mental illness. A sense of exclusion, injustice or just plain outrage is often the beginning of engagement with government.

The important distinction between communities of this kind and, for example, 'policy communities', is that policy communities are professionalised by continuing engagement with government, whereas communities based on identity or concern retain a strong sense of personal affiliation among their members. In relation to public policy, then, 'community' denotes groups of citizens who are interested in, or affected by, a particular issue. Some policy structures have a permanent place for community representatives (for example, community representatives may sit on consultative bodies). In many instances, though, 'the community' tends to be defined by the issue, so that, for example, a health issue might galvanise a quite different part of the community than a sports issue.

Community consultation enables a policy initiative or proposal to be 'road-tested' by giving affected members of the community the opportunity to comment on it. While the results of community consultation can be glossed over or ignored, the process requires agencies to define and try to reach groups that can be defined in many different ways—from personal attributes to residence in particular geographic locations.

The community has a warm and cuddly feel—in the abstract. The reality is that when the community is most engaged, it is also likely to be most critical of government. The closer to home (often literally) the issue happens to be, the more likely are so-called ordinary citizens to be concerned. Communities are not usually stirred up by trade policy negotiations, but even the most apathetic become engaged when, for example, a new motorway is proposed for their suburb.

The methods for reaching the community almost always result in those who feel most passionately about an issue becoming community spokespeople. Traditional democrats often discount the results of community consultation for this reason. If the community consists only of a few malcontents, they argue, why bother about it? This would, however, be a dangerous assumption to make. The views coming through could represent much more widely held opinions—the tip of the iceberg towards which the ship of state is heading. [1]

Involved stakeholders

A stakeholder is now commonly defined as a key individual or entity with an interest (a 'stake') in the outcome of a particular policy debate or decision. A stakeholder can also *be* a powerful interest, but this is not a necessary condition for stakeholder status. For those undertaking stakeholder analysis, the identity of the key players is often self-evident—so much so that their participation has become institutionalised through advisory bodies.

Advisory bodies have been familiar features of the bureaucratic landscape for many years and continue to play prominent roles in the definition of agendas and the administration of programs. Advisory bodies, if they are used well, allow governments to tap into a range of stakeholder communities, securing interest-based and knowledge-based reactions to proposals.

The term *'stakeholder engagement'* describes more active initiatives (by governments) to bring together groups of stakeholders, usually in response to a specific consultation exercise or policy need. From the perspective of those 'invited in', stakeholder engagement gives those affected by policy a sharper focus on their relationship to government and at least the beginnings of an entree into government itself. From government's perspective, to engage stakeholders means (or should mean) not just listening to them, but being prepared to take notice of them.

Powerful interests

At a minimum, governments must engage those whose cooperation is needed for the implementation of policy. Business, for example, was a key implementing agent of the Australian goods and services tax (GST). In this case, although the Tax Office was legally able to sanction non-complying businesses, in reality, there was a substantial interactive period after the passage of the legislation, during which business and the Tax Office grappled with the practical detail.

Planning agencies find themselves engaged with developers (and with the political executive) on a regular basis. Legislation prescribes these interactions and the level and circumstances in which they take place, but it is often the 'engagement' (information exchange, sometimes agreement making) around these matters that shapes the outcomes.

The extent to which interests should be included in the early stages of policy making (that is, before definite design characteristics have been decided on) is problematic. There is a danger that strong interests will fail to agree on a framework. The Rudd Government's process for developing policy to control carbon emissions was extensively consultative, but within specified values (that is, growth should be sacrificed as little as possible) and design parameters (an emissions trading scheme). On the other hand, an imposed framework might simply displace dissent to less public arenas.

Other government agencies

The landscape of government is populated by a bewildering diversity of public organisations. Indeed, for public servants contemplating engagement with the broader public, a key prerequisite is understanding and identifying the interests of other agencies that are involved. The Management Advisory Committee's *Connecting Government* describes a number of structures that can be used to bring different elements together, including the use of interdepartmental committees (IDCs), task forces and cross-agency partnerships (MAC 2004).

Task forces differ from IDCs, in that participants leave their home agency's priorities behind them and focus on solving a problem, usually in a short time frame. The Howard Government used task forces to bypass more conventional processes and to bring 'outsiders' into the heartland of bureaucratic policy development (Stewart and Maley 2007). In situations in which governance is evolving, rather than established, agencies often circle warily around each other, with little incentive to interact productively, unless (often) contingent factors serve to break the ice (see Stewart and Jones 2003). The risky activity of 'boundary riding' (talking across departmental boundaries) is essential for this type of engagement.

Summing up

Engagement (of those outside government in the policy process) is a difficult concept to visualise clearly. 'Ladders' of engagement are problematic, because techniques are not clearly differentiated from the relationships they serve. For example, 'consultation' can be equated with a two-way exchange of information and 'partnering' can be used to describe closer forms of involvement. Clearly, however, consultation (in the sense of ascertaining opinion) lies at the heart of all forms of engagement, however close (or distant) are the relationships implied.

It is suggested here that a significant characterising variable is the degree of power that is shared between those 'within' and those 'without' government. Power takes many forms; the key question is 'how much or how little' do I need to take into account the views of those I am consulting? From the perspective of those within government, the 'who' of engagement might involve individuals or groups that are close to the structures of executive government or those further away. Power to engage (or to withhold) does not, however, necessarily diminish as distance increases. The community can (on occasion) demand engagement, while (depending on context) agencies within government might not be able to insist on inclusion. The success of the public manager will depend on his or her ability to 'read' these contexts and structures.

Endnotes

[1] There are a number of manuals describing community consultation in detail, from a 'toolbox' perspective. One of the most comprehensive is *Best Value Victoria*: *Community consultation resource guide*, put out by the Victorian Local Governance Association and the Victorian Department of Local Government.

2. Why engage?

There are normative and practical arguments for engagement. The practical arguments relate to costs and benefits—always significant for practising managers. It is, however, equally important to consider the normative arguments (that is, why we should engage). Public managers might pride themselves on their practicality, but most want to understand (and where possible, to develop) the public interest dimensions of their profession.

The normative discussion inevitably takes us beyond the policy process as such, into the realms of the relationship between citizen and state. The normative arguments for enhanced citizen participation have been well set out by Fung (2006). According to this line of thought, engagement helps to overcome democratic deficits that have emerged in the functioning of modern states.

These deficits occur at four key points in the system: 1) between the interests of citizens and the preferences they express; 2) between citizens and their representatives; 3) between representatives and the policies that are really produced by the Executive; and 4) between the Executive and the outcomes that are produced. Consultative, participatory and deliberative forums provide mechanisms for decreasing these deficits and, in some ways, for bypassing them all together.

Addressing deficit one: articulating preferences through deliberation

Deliberation means that preferences are formed (and changed) through discussion with others. Forms of deliberative preference articulation—such as deliberative polling and citizens' juries—enable citizens to come together, debate and issue recommendations on nominated policy issues. In this way, citizens do not simply articulate interests, but form new preferences as a result of debate. As Rawls puts it:

> The definitive idea for deliberative democracy is the idea of deliberation itself. When citizens deliberate, they exchange views and debate their supporting reasons concerning public policy questions. They suppose that their political opinions may be revised by discussion with other citizens and therefore these opinions are not simply a fixed outcome of their existing private or non-political interests. (Rawls 1997:772)

Note Rawls' emphasis on the implications—practical and theoretical—of citizens' involvement in deliberation. In so doing, they 'suppose' that their opinions can be changed as a result of the process.

By seeing interests as fluid (rather than fixed), deliberative techniques allow for (and encourage) free-ranging forms of debate. In turn, the idea of consultation as discerning or discovering views that are already held is transcended: it is held that views are formed through practice. Indeed, in its more radical forms, deliberative democracy transcends even the necessity for consultation, because citizens make decisions directly for themselves.

Addressing deficit two: revisiting representation

Where (as in Westminster systems) the political executive is drawn from the Parliament and, by definition, has sufficient control over the Parliament to pass a budget, the ability of members effectively to represent their constituents' interests in any meaningful way is almost completely negated. Elections are infrequent and representatives might be unduly swayed by special interests, or by the dictates of party loyalty, to the extent that they struggle to represent their constituents effectively.

Improving the accuracy of representation gives us a further argument for engagement in the political sphere. Regular consultation between representatives and constituents reinforces and refreshes the mandate that election implies. From this perspective, consultation directly improves democracy.

Addressing deficits three and four: holding public agencies accountable

While most decision making in modern polities is undertaken by public servants, there is little capacity (according to this perspective) for citizens, or their representatives, to hold public servants to account for these decisions. Parliamentary oversight is necessarily limited. Parliamentary estimates committees have some capacity to question public servants, although the field of questioning must, by tradition, be restricted to matters of administration, rather than of policy.

Ministers are technically accountable to Parliament for public service decisions, but in practice this accountability (at least, in the form of resignation) is rarely invoked. Mechanisms of administrative law have been devised to provide a pathway for review of executive decisions: to enable citizens affected by decisions to have them reviewed by tribunals and, where necessary, by the courts. These rights, however, are granted only in relation to individual decisions—matters of policy are excluded.

Against these deficits, forms of engagement that enable citizens to have a direct input into bureaucratic perspectives and decision making have a powerful role to play. They act as a corrective to the distortional tendencies inherent in the modern technocratic state. As Fung puts it:

On many state decisions, the interests of politicians and administrators may differ from those of the majority of citizens. It is difficult for citizens to use elections to compel politicians to act to advance popular interests rather than their elite ends when elections are uncompetitive, when narrow interests oppose diffuse ones, or when outcomes are difficult to monitor and assess. (Fung 2006:672)

By opening up channels of communication, engagement (at least potentially) brings fresh sources of information and new perspectives to bear on political forms of decision making. While lobbying brings pressure to bear at close quarters (and usually in secret), the more public processes of engagement also, over time, affect political agendas. Paul Sabatier's (1999) influential theory of coalition formation highlights the way in which the perceived need to influence government enhances learning—that is, finding new ways of perceiving problems—as well as catalysing the formation of new alliances. These processes have been shown to have a direct bearing on the content of political and, eventually, institutional (public service) policy agendas.

In sum, then, greater citizen engagement augments the often faltering processes of basic democracy by:

- counteracting the unbalanced influence of elite opinion
- bringing stronger pressures of accountability to bear
- facilitating the building of coalitions for agenda development.

Are democratic deficits overplayed?

Against these views, a number of theorists have suggested that these arguments are overplayed and that the normal institutions of representative democracy, as we see them operate, are sufficiently democratic for our purposes. They make the point that attempts to augment these institutions with additional, more far-reaching forms are either doomed to ineffectiveness or, worse, can actually hinder democracy.

It is true that in theoretical terms, representative democracy does not require direct engagement from citizens. The eighteenth-century conservative British political theorist Edmund Burke was of the view that a political representative owes his constituents 'not his industry only, but his judgment; and he betrays, instead of serving you, if he sacrifices it to your opinion'. [1]

In the practical sense, it could be argued that representative democracy came into being precisely in order to overcome the problems posed by direct engagement. The size and complexity of modern states make the 'active voice' assemblies of Periclean Athens, or the town meetings of early New England, impractical as decision-making bodies, even in very localised contexts.

As we have seen, the nature of the relationship between elected representative and citizens is clearly complex, with many possibilities for 'disconnections' to occur. It is clearly impossible for one member to represent voters' preferences in any direct sense and the idea (or ideal) of delegation does not work well when elections are infrequent.

From the perspective of engagement, however, there might be more happening than meets the eye. Engagement between citizens and their elected representatives is an under-studied field of Australian political science. There are fewer safe seats than in the past and few local members can afford to neglect their constituency. The demands constituents place on their local member, whether or not they are members of the governing party, are diverse and, often, exacting. Representatives are expected to attend functions, open shows, kiss babies and, when required, make representations to ministers on behalf of constituents. Parties disendorse 'good local members' at their peril.

Institutionalists such as Goodin argue that, in any case, concentrating too much on day-to-day politics misses the point. These theorists point out that basic, systemic models of political behaviour do not capture the richness of overarching and intermediating structures and processes (Goodin 2003). Politicians often pretend that they can start anew with public policy, but the results of past choices are hardwired into the structures of the State. Institutional theory attempts to capture this complexity.

Institutions are, broadly speaking, the sets of rules that condition people's behaviour. These rules are as much implicit as they are explicit. As defined by March (1989), institutions embrace routines, procedures, technologies and roles (such as those of the labour market or of public education) and are built up over many years.

In decision-making terms, these institutions have been rightly described as 'mobilising bias'—that is, they confer access and give decision-making form to some perspectives and deny others (Bachrach and Baratz 1962). They are, however, certainly not unchanging or unchangeable. Recent work on policy values shows the extent to which institutions (and public agencies operating within them) can incorporate new and often incompatible values (Thacher and Rein 2004; Stewart 2006). When they escape these mediating mechanisms, value conflicts are powerful engines of change. Indeed, the beauty of politics is that it provides the energy to overhaul quite entrenched institutional forms.

We do not know whether improvements to the operations of representative democracy or moves towards more participatory forms are likely to yield more responsive or more informed policy. The two theories—representative versus participatory democracy—are constructions based on norms, not hypotheses that can be tested. As Sabatier has argued, these positions can be more usefully thought of as lenses, rather than theories. At the academic and the practitioner levels, it is a matter of applying the lens that seems to most usefully illuminate the reality under review (Sabatier 1999). As Fung points out, there is a need to democratise the *policy* process; the issue is how best to accomplish this goal.

Why engage? The policymaking perspective

In relation to policy making, the normative, democratically oriented literature shades into (and often overlaps with) more practically grounded analyses, which canvass the 'why engage' question from the perspective of costs and benefits, advantages and disadvantages.

In policymaking terms, the benefits relate to:

- improving information flows
- seeking a diversity of views
- obtaining early warning of problems
- tapping into community resources
- political management.

Improving information flows

Many public managers might wonder why one would choose to expand the flow of information coming into government. There would already appear to be ample opportunities for those with something to say, or simply some kind of grievance, to access politicians, particularly those at the local level.

On the other hand, public bureaucracies are often shielded from the communities they serve. While public servants who deal directly with the public often have a good sense of what people want, those further up the hierarchy must direct their attention upwards and outwards, rather than downwards. For most citizens, most of the time, the fleeting moment of choice when they cast their ballot is as close as they get to exercising political influence.

Ministers with executive power are busy, preoccupied and often remote figures. Ministerial advisers, dedicated to advancing the political interests of their bosses, control access to them. Indeed, as close gatekeepers, they can fashion the policy agenda by facilitating access by some groups at the expense of others (Ryan 1995). These advisers must be the eyes and ears of ministers, but at the same time, they have been known to shield their ministers from accountability through the mechanism of 'plausible deniability' (Tiernan 2007; Stewart 2008a). Ministers, in turn, are subject to unremitting pressures. The type and quality of information reaching decision makers are subject to significant distortion in these situations.

Open consultative channels provide at least the possibility for the views of service deliverers, clients and consumers to reach decision makers. More participatory forms of governance bring these views into the heartland of government itself. To the extent that information flow of this kind becomes routine, rather than being dependent on particular consultative occasions or pretexts, the more likely it is that policy will adjust to circumstances in real time.

Enhancing diversity

Consultation, even community consultation, does not automatically enhance diversity of input into decision making. The 'community' is an elusive concept that can often be defined only in relation to the policy issue itself. This 'community of fate' (Catt and Murphy 2003) might be coextensive with the general public or it might be a particular subset of that public (for example, the community of people living adjacent to a proposed development).

The distortional aspects of 'open' consultation are well known. Those engaged in consultative processes are likely to be better educated and more articulate than their fellows and often have powerful views to push as well. One Dutch consultation (on urban regeneration) found that almost all the participants were white, middle class and male (van de Meer and Edelenbos 2006). In the Australian context, studies have found that conventional consultation excludes 'hard-to-reach' groups such as migrants and Aboriginal people (Cameron and Grant-Smith 2005).

On the other hand, policy advisers who are wise to these traps can enrich policy making by deliberately seeking out other views. Policies that target particular groups are a case in point. Policy makers who talk to drug addicts and drug dealers, for example, as well as to professionals in the field, might find that their initial assumptions or preconceptions—indeed, the way they construct the issues in their minds—need to be adjusted in the light of 'reality testing' in the field. Governments have found that successful policy often depends on close and continuing contact with marginalised groups. To this end, Australian governments have funded, among others, peak bodies representing refugees, people with AIDS and sex workers (Sawer 2002).

Policy communities that privilege certain forms of knowledge can be daunting for outsiders to penetrate. (If you don't understand the acronyms, you are probably an outsider.) Indeed, it seems to have been with the idea of breaking through existing, bureaucratic mind-sets that Prime Minister John Howard brought executives of not-for-profit groups into the inner circles of policy making during the production of the *McClure Report* into changes to the welfare system (Stewart and Maley 2007).

Early warning of problems

Complex systems go wrong in unexpected ways. Hierarchical organisations notoriously quash warnings and dissent from within, making them vulnerable to unpleasant surprises. Where 'capture' by external interests has occurred, decision making can be distorted in ways that are no longer clearly visible to those within the organisation. Particular ways of proceeding have simply become institutionalised, without appropriate risk analysis being done.

By engaging with outsiders, managers might not only uncover new sources of intelligence, they might gain a warrant for speaking truth 'up the line'. Regulators, such as the Australian Competition and Consumer Commission (ACCC), are increasingly discovering the importance of soliciting and using personalised forms of knowledge—for example, by encouraging consumers and insiders to report price-fixing arrangements. The Australian National Audit Office, too, makes use of intelligence from the field.

Tapping into community resources

Professionals tend to view 'the community' as an amorphous mass of mainly untutored individuals. Every community, however, contains people whose knowledge is of the utmost value to public servants. Retirees, for example, are an often-overlooked source of wisdom. Many have 'seen it all before', but their successors might be all the better for knowing that they are neither the first (nor the last) to embark on a particular endeavour.

Partnering with community groups (for example, through environmental programs such as Landcare) brings not only the budgetary blessings of volunteer labour, but the immediate, practical knowledge of those directly involved with the issues at hand. Implementation is a detailed business. It cannot be managed solely from Canberra or, for that matter, from state capitals.

Greater problem-solving capacity

Complex problems pose difficulties for hierarchical organisations. Bureaucracy rests on the functional division of responsibility—this is the source of its well-known efficiency. Where issues are well structured and are not subject to rapid change, conventional bureaucracy is highly effective.

There are, however, many fields in which these conditions do not hold. Environmental questions continually challenge us, precisely because our conventional bureaucracies divide 'the environment' up according to developmental priorities. Thus, agricultural departments help farmers to produce. It is with difficulty that they become departments of sustainable farming (although there has been remarkable movement in this direction). Generally speaking, bureaucracy prefers to put 'production' in one box and 'the environment' in another, relying on interdepartmental mechanisms of various kinds to resolve coordination problems.

As Australians are discovering, water management is particularly challenging because of the complex, multi-level negotiations that must be undertaken if change is to be successful. Not only governments, but communities, individuals and their collective organisations are involved. Social policy, too, if it is to be at all sensitive to individual circumstance, must be alive to the possibilities of co-production. Fung, citing Booher and Innes (2002), puts the matter well:

> [P]roblems that involve interdependent actors who have diverse interests, values, and experiences, such as in many kinds of natural resource management and economic development problems, have often proven resistant to traditional top-down, state-centred mechanisms and methods. (Fung 2006:681)

If collective action is to apply at all in these situations, it must be inter-organisational and it must engage interests in new ways. The resulting configurations will need to be based on networked information and decision-making flows, with new relationships between 'top', 'middle' and 'bottom'. There are numerous examples where we see the beginnings of these new forms, although in some cases their development has been delayed by centralising tendencies and in others by the adaptive prowess of existing public agencies (Stewart and Jones 2003).

Problem solving through enhanced learning

How do participatory forms improve on the learning implied by conventional politics? Dutch network theoreticians have arguably gone furthest in identifying the nature of the problem-solving capacities of interactive networks. Thus, solutions are reached not by conventional means, but by tapping into 'on-the-ground' or 'real-time' perspectives.

Edelenbos describes the theory of interactive learning in this way:

> Process-oriented policy making is directed towards the design and management of a process which allows these actors and their problems and solutions to interact, to learn from one another, and to derive new, shared problems and solutions. (Edelenbos 1999:570)

It should be emphasised, however, that these theoretical arguments are only as good as the practical realities they make possible. It is also true that the academic literature must be sensitive to meta-evaluation, to learning, not simply from essentialist prescription, but from lived experience.

Political management

While it is not often brought out into the open, the main motivation to engage might have little to do with knowledge, resources or problem solving. For the practising manager, consultation will often be related to the need to craft politically acceptable compromises, or to keep interests with the power to frustrate a particular policy 'inside' rather than 'outside' the tent.

More generally, consultation is a good way to 'keep track' of the needs and opinions of key interests. Reporting against service levels, for example, is an excellent way of highlighting achievements and marketing change, and of matching expectations with deliverables. For service providers at the local level (for example, local government), regular consultation of this kind kills several birds with one stone.

Summing up

There are strong normative and practical reasons for those in government to engage with citizens. The normative arguments relate to the tendency for modern representative democracies to become distant from citizens. Very often, these 'democratic deficits' can be addressed only by deliberately restructuring or otherwise improving channels of communication between citizens and their elected representatives on the one hand and between citizens and executive decision makers on the other. Engagement improves legitimacy for these reasons.

In the practical sense, there are benefits from engagement for public managers employed in policy making and in administration. Engagement improves the likelihood of successful policy by enhancing information flow and encouraging diversity of policy advice. Of course, there are risks associated with engagement as well as rewards. Consulting the 'community' might privilege some groups at the expense of others. Nevertheless, in many fields (particularly those where many different kinds of actions must be coordinated), the benefits of engagement would appear to outweigh the costs.

Endnotes

[1] From Burke's 'Speech to the electors of Bristol' (1774), *The works of the Right Honourable Edmund Burke*, Vol 2, New York, Wells and Lilly, 1826 [available in digitised form via Google Books, http://books.google.com.au/]

3. The 'how' of engagement: contexts and achievements

While the rhetorical literature is abundant, it is difficult to obtain from it an overall sense as to what is happening in relation to engagement. The OECD's (2001) comprehensive comparative study suggests that most countries have surmounted at least the first rung of the consultation ladder. Citizens' rights to information are routinely enshrined in freedom of information acts (although the practical workings of these pieces of legislation are, of course, another matter).

Beyond this level, tracking achievement is most easily done by surveying the practical purposes for which engagement has been used and describing the development of the techniques that have underpinned its advance. The intention here is not to present a description of the many techniques that are available. Rather, it is to suggest how techniques and formats relate to the nature of the relationships that engagement fosters and beyond these relationships, to the values that they represent, and the purposes they aim to achieve.

I proceed by considering engagement in relation to the broad categories and purposes outlined in Chapters 1 and 2: first, consultation and the various kinds of information exchange that facilitate it; second, the use of engagement for purposes of conflict resolution; and third, the creation of participatory governance.

Consultation

If the number of manuals and handbooks was an indication of the extent to which consultation was really carried out, we might conclude that the practice has an assured place in policy making. This is clearly not the case: many policies are too political, too hastily assembled or simply too difficult to explain, to reconcile with the demands of proper consultation. Consultation requires considerable expertise and experience to organise successfully and many governments simply do not have the people to do the work. Nevertheless, consultation guides and manuals do, at least, tell us what governments think consultation is about, even if the reality is far less impressive.

In Australia, state and local governments have produced the most highly developed consultation manuals. While described by Catt and Murphy as 'menu lists' for consultation, these guides (at least implicitly) draw from the lessons of experience, as well as the dictates of commonsense. One of the most highly evolved practice manuals on community consultation was published under the auspices of the Local Government Division of the Victorian Department of Infrastructure and the Victorian Local Government Association.

The Victorian Local Government Association's manual identifies a range of consultation interfaces, ranging from the strategic to the operational. We might call this 'guided' consultation, in which the consultation agenda is firmly established in the context of implementation. As the guide puts it, '[c]onsultation should take place early in the implementation of…specific services, so that councils can be sure that the principles of quality and cost standards, accessibility, responsiveness and continuous improvement are informed by consultation' (VLGA n.d.).

The Management Advisory Committee's influential publication *Connected Government* emphasises the importance of professional appreciation of the constraints on engagement (for example, the need to maintain cabinet confidentiality) while consulting as widely as practicable (MAC 2004:Ch. 6). 'Whole of government'—that is, achieving outcomes by combining and coordinating previously disparate public resources—is particularly engagement intensive.

The OECD consultation manual is less specific, but highlights the importance of building an overall consultation framework, highlighting the objectives that the consultation is designed to serve and choosing appropriate tools to achieve the objectives. The manual stresses the importance of generating and maintaining trust, delivering on promises and, above all, looking at the occasion from the citizen's perspective (OECD 2001).

Information exchange

While all forms of engagement involve information exchange, it is undoubtedly engagement with the community that has brought about the most innovation. We might summarise the techniques that have been developed as 'putting out' ideas in a way that elicits information either about the ideas directly or about the community's attitude towards them. It is not, however, only community consultation that has been important in this context. A growing literature points to the importance of the information being appropriate to the purpose and the background of the participants, whoever they are.

Evidence from web sites and recent experience suggests that policy makers are prepared to engage outsiders in increasingly flexible ways. According to the widely used 'policy cycle', consultation is a phase in the process that occurs after policy analysis and before decision making. While this fits some types of consultation—for example, Treasury consulted with stakeholders before introducing recent legislation to curb insider trading—there are many others where consultation is used for other purposes. The Rudd Government's 2020 Summit (April 2008), for example, was aimed at consolidating the government's agenda, while giving the impression that it was prepared to go 'outside' the usual communities of interest to gather ideas.

Reductions in the cost of consultation have probably done more than any other single change to encourage its wider use. E-government has made it much easier to distribute information relating to the more conventional forms of consultation, such as exposure drafts and calls for comments on particular pieces of legislation. On the other hand, as we shall see, public servants have been slower than politicians to exploit the networking opportunities of new technology.

Green papers (setting forth ideas for discussion) and white papers (reflecting final decisions) are traditional staples of 'inquiring' modes of public policy. Newer forms of engagement stress the relevance of techniques and relationships that produce forms of knowledge that are often more personal and concrete than the rational model, and that actively involve the community in revelatory and/or deliberative ways.

Photographs

A specific example will be useful here. [1] A council in rural New South Wales, using a state government grant, employed community development officer Joy Engelman to try to revive flagging townships in the area. To do this, she needed to consult with communities in the shire about what was important to them. Engelman contacted local clubs to help her organise meetings in each of the towns. She used these meetings to get ideas from as broad a base as possible. She also wanted to recruit a core group of volunteers in each town to push the ideas forward. It was sometimes hard going, but she found her six volunteers in each town.

Engelman's next step was to find out what the important features of each town were for the people who lived there. Taking photos was the key here. She had three of her volunteers get out and about with a camera. They took photos of six things they liked and six they disliked. The photos were displayed at a public meeting organised by a fourth member of the team. When they came across something that needed improvement, Engelman told the relevant council people about it. 'For example,' she says:

> [T]here was an uneven bit of pavement in the main street of one of the towns. It had been bugging people for years. I got in touch with the town's engineers and it was fixed. That sort of thing doesn't cost much, and it builds people's confidence in the program, that it will actually achieve something (personal communication, late 1999).

Storytelling and anecdote

As the chair of a parliamentary committee investigating a social policy issue put it, 'Getting the data is important. But what really communicates a human sense of the issues is when people sit around a table and tell their stories.' [2] Stories or anecdotes are used as the 'medium' of engagement in a number of contexts, ranging from program evaluation to organisational development. Anecdotes might be no more than glimpses of a single episode or revelations of mood, but they are distinguished from opinion in the sense that they report a reality with which others can engage. As one practitioner put it, 'Stories lead to stories. Opinions lead to other opinions.' [3]

The theoretical case for the use of anecdotes in organisational settings derives from a number of sources, including complexity theory (see Snowden and Boone 2007). In many situations, there is no 'right' answer and learning to 'think small' in appropriate ways can be of more practical utility than searching for holistic (and probably wrong) solutions. There is also a hint of the work of the American organisation theorist Karl Weick, who notes that, far from being the rational machines some imagine, organisations depend for their effectiveness on their capacity to move beyond the bland. Effective organisations are, in fact, 'garrulous, clumsy, wandering and grouchy' (Weick 2008).

Electronic networking

In a modern democracy, the channels of communication are rarely silent, largely because of the ubiquity and power of modern media. When governments wish to influence citizens (as distinct from giving them information), the provision of information takes more calculated forms. The presence of citizens (as voters) shapes activity throughout the Executive, most strongly at the interface between the political and the bureaucratic executives. Governments must find ways of communicating with voters that give effect to a compelling narrative or story.

Governments (and oppositions) have a strong political motivation to track the opinions of citizens through opinion polls and focus groups. The importance of public relations produces a large, vaguely delineated area where genuine information overlaps with political merchandising. The marketing of new policies is carefully pre-tested—a useful step in implementation. In the lead-up to an election year, the problems become more pressing. Governments can use focus groups to design advertising campaigns. If the flow of information is one way, its effect will, nevertheless, be carefully monitored, measured and, where necessary, reacted to.

While hard data are difficult to come by, departments and agencies appear not to emphasise opinion-related information to nearly the same extent as the political parts of the Executive. 'Evidence' is usually construed as factual information obtained through research and analysis. When the Treasury famously ignored 'anecdotal evidence' of a gathering recession in the early 1990s, interest rates (then set by political decision makers) were arguably kept too high for too long as a result.

Communication technologies offer the promise of online canvassing of opinion. The OECD, for example, makes extensive use of e-consultation in preparing guides and manuals. Apart from individual use of opinion sites and chat rooms, however, examples of public servants devising versions of these technologies for professional use are rare. Web sites enable agencies to inform users of their programs, tell them about the latest developments and, where feedback is sought, to consult with users. The OECD (2001:51) reported that all members were 'making significant efforts to bring their governments and their citizens on line'. Only some countries, however, had made concerted efforts to establish standards for the type and quality of information provided through web sites.

Whether e-governance should be seen as a means for achieving traditional strategies more cost effectively or is itself at least potentially transformative has excited widespread debate (Dugdale 2008). Empirical work suggests that even techniques of discussion and debate, when employed in official or quasi-official contexts, are constrained in character. Chen (2004), for example, found that discussion lists in the field of political science remained tied to (and expressive of) existing institutional structures.

The use of information and communication technologies to help further community development has a patchy history. Sutcliffe and Richardson (2004) found that without prior investment in the development of social capital, little could be achieved through the use of technology alone. As Joseph (2004) notes, the problem is that the role of information in public policy is poorly understood. Information is not primarily about technology, but creating forms of information that will be useful.

Campaigning politicians have been quick to tap the interactive possibilities of networking and old dogs (or their staffers) quickly learn new tricks. A Facebook site is a must for the enterprising politician. In policy-related fields, information and communication technologies have revolutionised the often-cumbersome procedures of traditional information exchange. Lists of email addresses, grouped according to the need at hand, streamline interactions with stakeholders.

From community perspectives, the instant communication of email helps concerned groups keep in touch and respond quickly to developments. As soon as there is a change somewhere in the network, the others can be 'onto it' instantly. South Sydney's REDwatch exists specifically to monitor what governments do. 'Government knows that REDwatch is on top of all the changes and that they will be called to account' (Inner Sydney Regional Council for Social Development Inc. 2008:10).

Fusing ideas and support

Where the context is settled (that is, a document is produced and reviewed on a regular basis), gathering responses boils down to letting people know that the process is under way. Where the context is not settled (for example, gathering views and opinions about the future of a heritage area in a town), the choices multiply. Often, processes are required (such as meetings with community groups) to get things going, before information-gathering techniques (such as focus groups) can be employed.

Depending on their resources, governments can employ broadly based, facilitated processes that draw out community sentiment, meaning and memory (such as 'charettes'). A charrette is a kind of workshop used to bring ideas, experts and the community together. The output is a design, plan or description. The charette arose originally from the design field, where architects, developers and community members would meet together to produce broad design solutions that contained a realistic depiction of the future. Typically, in policy-related charettes, a team of experts meets with community groups and with stakeholders to gather information on issues that face the community. This information is then used, in a transparent way, to produce a vision or general direction that reflects the values and priorities of those who are most affected.

Alternatively, those designing consultation can opt for a more strategic process that links to a community future or vision. Producing community visions helps people to describe and to define what is important to them. These are commonly large-group processes that can operate over many contexts and employ a variety of techniques. What is vital to the 'vision' is the articulation of values. Palerang Council, for example, used visioning workshops to tell it what it no doubt already knew: that most people saw the natural environment as their main reason for living in the area (Rogers 2006).

Deliberative forums

Deliberative forms and forums have 'star quality' in the annals of engagement and have been heavily discussed in the academic literature. It is, however, difficult to ascertain the extent to which deliberation is: a) really occurring; and b) what difference it is making. The literature tends to feature examples rather than inventories. A rare exception is Lyn Carson's (2006) inventory of Australia's (limited) practice. The situation is further complicated by the claims made by the growing number of firms offering to organise or facilitate deliberative events (see for example, America speaks, <www.americaspeaks.org>). Deliberation and deliberative techniques and software are being sold by business and not-for-profits to government, billed as mechanisms for accessing public opinion within wide-ranging citizen-engagement strategies (see, for example, Lukensmeyer and Torres 2006).

Deliberative forums, such as citizens' juries, have been used to access groups often marginalised by conventional consultation. An Australian example, the Parra Youth Matters jury, brought together 17 young jurors from an area of western Sydney. The experience helped the participants to formulate their views on a number of issues, including the media. As a pilot project, the jury suggested pathways for aligning deliberation among young people with continued community building (Carson et al. 2004).

Published examples of deliberative techniques in use suggest that they are used most extensively in relation to planning, transport and civic issues. For example, the San Diego County Regional Airport Authority (as reported by Lukensmeyer and Torres 2006) conducted a series of six citizen dialogues on the future of the city's airport in an attempt to balance the interests of citizens with those of visitors. The dialogues were interactive and structured around real alternatives. The exercise showed how deeply citizens were divided on the question of values. Some welcomed a multipurpose 'aeroplex' to accommodate a wide range of uses, whereas others 'were deeply opposed to the congestion and development patterns associated with the proposal'. The conclusion drawn was that any decision-making mode that did not take citizen input seriously would be deeply resented (Lukensmeyer and Torres 2006:27).

Because deliberative practice can occur in many ways, it is often difficult to disentangle 'ordinary' consultation from deliberation. For example, the process of 'visioning' is potentially deliberative, but in practice, visionary documents or strategies (such as the 10-year vision for the British National Health Service) incorporate input from a variety of groups that have been consulted: the 'deliberation' has occurred within the organisation preparing the words (see the interim report at <www.dh.gov.uk>). Hendriks (2002), reporting on the progress of citizens' forums in Europe and North America, notes that these processes are employed as an adjunct to conventional decision-making processes, rather than as an alternative to them.

In Australia, deliberative forums—such as the Hawke Government's National Economic Summit of 1983 and the 1998 Convention on the Republic—have been used for purposes of symbolic agenda setting and political management. If Australia is ever to become a republic it seems that some kind of prolonged public deliberation (leading to the necessary referendum) will be required. Australia's original constitutional conventions of the 1890s would today be regarded as forms of deliberative democracy.

The British Columbia Citizens Assembly on Electoral Reform, held in July 2003, showed the power of assemblies, selected on principles of stratified random sampling, to generate consensus on complex and deep questions of political organisation. Although a subsequent referendum to change the electoral system was narrowly lost, the assembly played a key role in legitimating the case for change (Sharman 2006). In the United States, the Utah Growth Summit played a significant agenda-setting role by engaging the public in discussing growth scenarios and outlining problem areas (Walters et al. 2000).

Deliberation would appear to have a role to play in contentious policy issues, where citizens must incorporate scientific or other professional evidence into their thinking. Proposals to recycle sewage appear to lend themselves to precisely this type of forum, although, so far, no Australian government has been courageous enough to convene one. In relation to policy, one well-documented Australian example involved a citizen's forum that was convened in 2000 (under the sponsorship of the NSW Government) to discuss container deposit legislation (Hendriks 2002). In this case, however, reconciling the views of business interests with those of the community (post deliberation), proved a major stumbling block to further progress.

Dealing with conflict

Governments do not like conflict, and indeed some types of engagement represent attempts to overcome or to defuse particularly fractious issues. Consultative forums—such as the Sydney Airport Consultative Committee set up in the 1990s in response to aircraft noise—can be used to legitimate decision making by bringing those previously excluded into the fold (Stewart and Jones 2003). Many consultative forums owe their genesis to this type of conflict resolution, but later become permanent features of the landscape.

Negotiated agreements

Regional Forest Agreements (RFAs) have been much discussed in the Australian literature. While their substantive effects (in terms of the future of old-growth forests) have been greatly disputed, the verdict in relation to governance has been much more positive (see Stewart and Jones 2003; Mercer 2000).

As governance mechanisms, the RFAs brought peace to a highly conflict-ridden arena. This was achieved through an extensive process of negotiated trade-offs, brokered at a high level, but with the local details worked out in conjunction with affected interests. The willingness of stakeholders to form part of the process was crucial to its durability. As Stewart and Jones noted, the ideological distance between the greens and their opponents widened as one journeyed south. It was only when the balance of power between interests allowed for negotiation and change that institutional biases towards development were redressed.

Committees of inquiry

It is easy to be cynical about committees and commissions of inquiry. Although politicians resort to them for many reasons, one important motivation is in order to defuse a significant scandal. The Cole Commission of Inquiry into the Australian Wheat Board, which proved ultimately to be a harbinger of the end for the Howard Government, was established in response to persistent opposition questioning and public concern about sanction-busting sales of Australian wheat to Iraq.

Many commissions, however, have been epoch making, precisely because they have brought out, in a public way, events and concerns that would otherwise have festered in silence. The Royal Commission into Aboriginal Deaths in Custody and the Wood Royal Commission into the NSW Police Force are obvious examples. Royal commissions do not always enable governments to control the issue. As Scott Prasser (2006) observes, they 'have a habit of biting the very governments that appoint them'.

The framework of royal commissions is judicial and it is because of the perceived integrity and independence of those chairing them that the proceedings attract considerable attention, and the recommendations carry considerable weight, even if most remain unimplemented. Commissions of this kind are investigatory rather than consultative bodies, although some (such as the Royal Commission into Australian Government Administration) do have consultative elements.

Policy-related committees of inquiry (executive and parliamentary) also range widely. The process is usually open and anyone may put in a submission. Clearly, though, the more specialised the inquiry, the more likely it is that submissions will be received from key stakeholders and subsequent deliberations will take place in relatively closed forums. The Garnaut reports into emissions trading are a significant contemporary example of this kind of inquiry.

Inquiries are versatile and some have certainly been commissioned to deliver (and to legitimate) a preordained result. The Uhrig Inquiry, for example, brought in an external figure (a businessman trusted by the government) to drive through a series of changes to the governance of statutory bodies (Commonwealth of Australia 2003).

Inquiries can contextualise an agenda for change that goes well beyond their terms of reference. Originally intended to smooth the regulatory path for business, the *Uhrig Report* provided a rationale for bringing the administration of welfare closer to the departmental heartland (Grant 2005).

Creating participatory governance

'Participatory governance' denotes forms of governance in which non-governmental actors (usually 'citizens') are empowered to use the resources of the State to make decisions about matters that directly concern them. For empirical researchers, however, it has proved an elusive quarry. At times, it seems a reality; at others, no more than a chimera—a weird and (possibly) mythical hybrid.

Within the academic literature, there is a degree of ambivalence displayed towards the mapping of participatory governance. On the one hand, we are told that new (or newish) forms of governance are bringing new players and processes into what were previously hierarchical governing arrangements. As Ian Marsh (2002:3) puts it, 'The vocabulary of governance reflects new interdependencies between the political leadership, public administration and the community...It reflects the new salience of strategic policy-making and the new contexts and pressures shaping agenda development'. If this is so, however, it implies that engagement is developing spontaneously, independently of the wishes of public managers.

The problem with this literature is that we can never be quite sure whether it is describing something that is really happening or using a particular perspective to write about something that has always been present. Policy networks (where participants have a common interest) have been a staple of analysis for many years. At times, the more recent network literature seems more exhortation than fact. The implications for practitioners are also difficult to unravel.

If engagement is an irresistible force, the task for practitioners is one of adapting to it. Experience 'on the ground', however, suggests that participatory forms do not come easily. When they emerge spontaneously, they are often informal and ephemeral. When they are 'designed' deliberately by public servants, their sustainability and effectiveness depend on active strategies to keep them going.

Examining a number of networked initiatives in Queensland, Keast and Brown (2006) found that the sustainability of these arrangements depended heavily on the involvement of central government agencies, as well as the commitment of a number of key players, often at middle-management level, determined to do the hard work of keeping network members engaged and interested.

Rather than seeing networked governance as a kind of meta-force, it might make more sense to see it as the product of specific developments. The demand for networked governance reflects a number of trends—increasing complexity, certainly, as cities are impacted by the competitive demands of globalising economies. Developments in public administration, however, have also played their role. Partnerships between the public and private sectors in financing development, for example, have become more important, as government has itself become less willing to assume the financial risks involved.

Participatory governance has also assumed an increasingly high profile in the administration of development, where it is often found that working through government agencies leads to waste and corruption. In this context, participatory governance is intended deliberately to give those who would normally lack power in governance (such as women and the rural poor) more say over the expenditure of funds.

While Australia is not normally thought of as a developing country, we do have some examples of exceptional social and economic deprivation. The continuing problems of Aboriginal communities, which experience rates of disease and social dysfunction far higher than those of non-Indigenous Australians, have led to a number of experiments in governance, including forms of self-government or self-management for Aboriginal communities.

Two forms of participatory governance have received useful empirical coverage:

- partnerships in service delivery
- multi-actor policy making.

Partnerships in service delivery

Outsourced forms of service delivery provide rich opportunities for participatory forms of governance. Whether these forms emerge as true partnerships or as more instrumental forms of engagement bounded solely by contracts depends on the overarching values and priorities of the funding agencies.

In the United Kingdom, the years of New Labour brought about a wide variety of these collaborations, in the fields of social inclusion, crime management and neighbourhood development. The social inclusion policy is particularly instructive in this context, as citizens (in specified geographical areas) are engaged in co-delivering certain services.

Sullivan and Skelcher (2002) identify three modes of engagement:

- the strategic, in which broad directions are discussed and citizens are involved through peak bodies
- the sectoral, in which the focus is on the users and beneficiaries of particular services
- neighbourhoods, where the focus is on the participants themselves.

Policy settings—and the values they contain and project—are of particular importance in shaping the character of these collaborations. Work done by Stewart (2007) identifies three levels—the policy, managerial and administrative levels—in each of which participants must find communicative channels through which to deal with value conflicts.

Multi-actor (participatory) policy making

Described as a 'decentralised unitary state', the Netherlands provides many examples of efforts to improve the sense of 'public' ownership of decision making by encouraging the creation of localised, rather than central, steering. In a crowded country, the context is one of constant change and competition between interests for public and private space.

Interactive policy making is one form of this localised steering. It is defined as cooperation between governments, societal groups and citizens and is distinguished from public–private partnerships, which are focused on the development of particular products, in which risk, costs and benefits are shared (van de Meer and Edelenbos 2006:205).

Dutch commentators report on a range of projects that are managed through participatory processes such as networks (Kickert et al. 1997). The attraction of these arrangements is that they are adaptive over time—that is, if it does its job properly, the network will facilitate 'double-loop' learning, which can become the basis for true institutional transformation. Examples include Dutch spatial planning policy processes, where 'top-down' forms of decision making and direction have been complemented by local-level detail and process (van de Meer and Edelenbos 2006).

As noted earlier, whether these processes are transformative or not depends on the values, purposes and priorities of those involved. True participatory governance requires politicians and public officials to share some of their power over policy processes. In particular, it requires them to share information with citizens and to learn how to communicate with so-called ordinary citizens about complex questions.

In *Renegotiating the Environment*, Stewart and Jones (2003) showed how, in certain conditions, forms of environmental governance could emerge in which the key actions of policy took place at the 'mid level' (between the national and the local), but involving a number of organisational players. Similar developments have been recorded in catchment management and urban regeneration. Where participants can be brought together (or come together) on the basis of place, there is often a more enduring basis for participation than if the commonality is more abstract (see, for example, Reddel and Woolcock 2004).

Information exchange in these situations is often built around interactive forums (see, for example, Success Works 2002). Those working across boundaries talk, nurture and talk some more. More formal processes must also be employed, particularly mechanisms for recording decisions and agreements. These are, however, punctuation points, rather than outcomes. If decisions (or even understandings) are involved, there will often be continuing interactive flow in order to implement them.

Where conflict resolution forms part of the interaction, a range of skills and attributes that are analytical and personal is required. Practitioners stress the importance of engendering trust and of creating some form of initial structure to 'ground' initial efforts.

Participatory budgeting

Undoubtedly, the acid test of participation is budgeting. While interest in participatory budgeting is growing, [4] overall, governments continue to keep budget processes close to their chests. Local budgets (such as those of councils) might be discussed in community meetings and forums, but for reasons canvassed earlier in this chapter, such settings are rare at other levels of government.

At the state and Commonwealth levels, interests lobby ministers and treasurers, and many prepare budget submissions. It would, however, be stretching matters to call this engagement, or even consultation. Finance officers do not go out to communities to ask them what they would like in the budget. The communities would probably die of shock if they did.

The reality is that budgets are zero-sum games and—at least in executive-dominated systems such as Australia and New Zealand—the budget makers are able to shield the process from the pressures of competitive deal making. At the same time, budgets are the single biggest source of disaffection, setting-up consultative needs and pressures down the track.

The role of public servants

Is the management of engagement a core skill for public servants? If so, how much should they do directly and how much indirectly? The evidence is interesting on this point, in that public servants are at both ends of the innovative spectrum. They are still very much in the driving seat of what we might call 'standard' forms of engagement—that is, when there is a review of a specific piece of (relatively non-controversial) policy or legislation.

At the same time, it is public servants who play lead roles in participatory forms of community engagement where there is a strong element of innovation or, to put the matter more cynically, desperation. Public servants facilitated the Council of Australian Governments (COAG) field trial in western New South Wales (discussed in more detail in Chapter 5).

In other contexts, however, public servants are stepping back and outsourcing the management of engagement to consultants. Their expertise, often specialised, frees public servants for other tasks, while also giving a useful 'shield' between the raw politics of the issue and more formal departmental and cabinet processes.

In the Australian Capital Territory, consultants were brought in to massage community angst after a round of school closures in late 2006, through facilitating discussion on the fate of the school sites. Consultants were also used by the ACT Planning and Land Authority to facilitate discussion of the draft Planning and Development Bill (2006–07).

On the implementation side, the Commonwealth Department of Agriculture, Forests and Fisheries uses consultants to implement resource-sharing agreements—that is, the broad design of the policy is agreed on, but the detail requires negotiation and compromise and is facilitated by specialist consultants.

Deliberative forms might be the intellectual property of specific consultants or academics, working as consultants, might establish powerful fields of practice where political leadership is supportive. For example, between 2001 and 2005, Jeanette Hartz-Karp organised 36 deliberative projects for the WA Minister for Planning and Infrastructure. One of the most influential of these was the 'Dialogue with the City', an exceptionally wide-ranging and creative set of deliberative activities, culminating in the production of 'Network City: A community plan for Perth and Peel' (Government of Western Australia 2008).

Summing up

Engagement has expanded its reach as new techniques have been developed. It is, however, difficult to know the extent to which these enhanced capacities have been reflected in widespread application. There is no 'moving front' of engagement but, rather, a patchwork of initiatives, experiments and established routines. While governments perceive engagement favourably, practices reflect fundamental state structures and the incentives for political executives and bureaucracies to engage with the public. These incentives appear to operate most strongly at the local level, where issues play out in a particular geographic locality. At other levels, forms of networked governance have proved difficult to sustain. The evidence suggests that it is the need to resolve particular problems—such as conflict between interests or perceived inefficiency—that has driven the creation of more participatory structures and practices.

Endnotes

[1] Information for this case study comes from Joy Engelman's report *Cabonne Country* for Cabonne Council's Small Towns Development Project 1997–2000.

[2] From a speech given in Canberra by Annette Ellis MP on World Mental Health Day 10 October 2008.

[3] From consultant Mark Schenk, speaking at a workshop on Narrative Techniques for Business held in October 2008.

[4] See, for example, the Draft National Strategy for Participatory Budgeting put out by the United Kingdom's Department for Communities and Local Government in 2008.

4. What works for managers? Case studies from the field [1]

We have seen that initiatives of many kinds have been practised and reported on in the past 20 years. What is known, however, about what works for managers? Evaluations of engagement strategies from this point of view are rare. In part, this is because deciding how to evaluate a process is fraught with conceptual difficulties. What does a 'good' consultation or a 'good' deliberation look like? When making comparisons, there are few counterfactuals—most policy systems remain hierarchical, with participatory forms occurring at the margins: the Angostura bitters in the cocktail of administrative life.

For their part, agencies like to promote their successes, admitting (usually) only to minor flaws. In assembling the following cases, I have taken the view that it is more productive (although certainly not easier) to assemble case studies that demonstrate particular themes of engagement, rather than simply telling the story of what happened.

The raw material for the new cases presented here comes from a forum specially convened for the 'Dilemmas' project, held on 22 August 2008. The forum brought together practitioners, academics and representatives of community groups to discuss a range of cases chosen so as to bring out a broad range of engagement issues and problems, with an emphasis on the public management perspective. The results point to areas of significant achievement and also to emergent difficulties: the true 'dilemmas of engagement'.

Consultation for regulation

'Regulation'—that is, rules for the determination of behaviour—is not often considered along with engagement. Regulatory agencies, however, and agencies that develop policies in the field often have longstanding relationships with policy communities. Regulators need reliable information in order to formulate and implement policy. They are, in general, in a strong position vis-a-vis stakeholders, because of the specialised nature of the knowledge they possess. On the other hand, becoming too close to stakeholders runs the risk of 'capture'—that is, the agency's decisions are biased towards those it is charged with regulating. In this section, I consider case studies drawn from financial policy making (the Australian Treasury) and from the implementation field (the Australian Competition and Consumer Commission).

Formal and informal channels of consultation

Consultation in the financial sector involves a number of specialised industries, each well organised, well resourced and with good access to government and an understanding of government processes. The issues involved in financial sector regulation are complex and regulatory frameworks have profound effects on business practices and costs. Consequently, there are often demanding time lines for policy makers, especially when changes to prudential regulation are under consideration. In rising to the challenge of these demands, policy makers use two methods: formal (relating to the staged process of submission, analysis and response) and informal (relating to more nuanced, rapid and personal interactions with stakeholders).

The *Financial Sector Legislation Amendment (Review of Prudential Decisions) Act 2007* introduced reforms to improve the efficiency, transparency and consistency of processes for disqualifying individuals from operating financial sector entities and enhancing the accountability of the Australian Prudential Regulation Authority (APRA) for its decisions. There were strong reasons for the government to act and equally strong incentives for the industry to engage with the government. Moreover, in the wake of the Royal Commission into the HIH collapse and the government's 2006 Taskforce on Reducing Regulatory Burdens on Business, there was a compelling reform agenda to be addressed, involving balancing regulator independence and power on the one hand, and the need, on the other, for an appropriate process of decision review.

An initial consultation paper had proposed that the independent regulator, APRA, have a single general power to give directions to financial sector entities to address prudential risks. The paper also proposed to introduce merits review of APRA decisions by the Administrative Appeals Tribunal, where appropriate, consistent with Administrative Review Council guidelines. Submissions to government on the proposals queried the scope of APRA's direction power as well as how merits review would work in practice. There were 22 submissions received to this initial consultation paper. In May 2007, a second consultation paper was issued with revised proposals designed to address concerns raised by industry to the initial proposals. Thirteen submissions were received by the government, which broadly supported the revised proposals that subsequently formed the basis of the act that was passed by the Parliament.

In reaching this result, the Treasury stressed the importance of using formal and informal channels of consultation. Formal consultation establishes the general 'rules of the game' and ensures transparency and fairness for all stakeholders. Submissions are made publicly available, subject to confidentiality provisions and represent stakeholders' official views, communicated to their members and to government. It is, however, a static rather than a dynamic process: announced views are weighed up, there may be further informal consultations and adjustments to proposals may be made.

The formal process depends in important respects on an informal process of information exchange and discussion that provides additional flexibility.

Stakeholders are, in any case, in regular contact with policy advisers and the informal process provides for an extension of this contact. Informal industry engagement assists in:

- shaping how proposals should be framed for formal consultation
- clarifying views expressed in formal submissions
- conveying additional context for the government's approach and clarifying next steps
- identifying the potential for compromise and building consensus.

Groups outside the immediate policy community tend not to be actively involved in these processes. From one perspective, this could be viewed as a weakness, with consumer groups, for example, most unlikely to be consulted on the detail of financial sector reforms. On the other hand, highly technical matters often held no interest to non-professionals and, in the case of prudential regulation, the overarching public interest principle of maintaining robust regulatory processes had already been established and widely accepted. Moreover, consumer groups preferred to target higher-level issues. In dealing with detailed reform proposals, there was a narrower focus on crafting a result that would be effective and implementable by the industry and the regulator.

Public and non-public consultation

Consultation does not always have to be public to be effective, as the example of the Australian Competition and Consumer Commission (ACCC) demonstrates. The ACCC uses public and non-public forms of consultation in highly structured ways in order to maximise access to information from the field. These consultative arenas are legislatively mandated, but, over time, have evolved in ways that might have more general application.

The commission holds non-public consultations when it considers proposals for mergers and acquisitions and public consultations when mergers that would otherwise be anti-competitive are investigated to determine whether they should be authorised in the public interest. The commission also conducts public consultations when it applies public interest tests to applications by firms to register conduct that may be anti-competitive.

The commission is a statutory body governed by a board, comprising a chair, two deputy chairs, a number of full-time members and associate members. Its activities are based in Canberra and in Melbourne and it has offices in every state. Its work is largely mandated by the *Trade Practices Act 1974* and takes place in five main areas:

- consumer law
- mergers and acquisitions
- prices surveillance

- adjudication
- regulation of particular industries (for example, telecommunications).

The overall objective of the ACCC is to promote competition and fair trade in the marketplace to benefit consumers, businesses and the community. It also regulates national infrastructure services. Its primary responsibility is to ensure that individuals and businesses comply with the Commonwealth competition, fair-trading and consumer protection laws.

The ACCC's mode of engagement with stakeholders differs according to the type of activity it is regulating. Mergers, for example, involve the commission in extensive interaction with companies wishing to merge with or acquire others. The ACCC advises the firms concerned whether the proposal will adversely affect market competition. This is a form of non-public consultation. The commission has a clear decision to make: it must determine whether the proposed change is anti-competitive or not. It cannot make this decision, however, without obtaining information from the marketplace—from suppliers and customers, from rivals and supporters. Much of this information is highly commercially sensitive—hence the consultation, while wide ranging in its contours and purposes, is not publicly reported. The case of Qantas's proposed merger with Air New Zealand shows these processes in action.

In 2003, Qantas and Air New Zealand approached the commission regarding plans to merge the two airlines. This was disallowed on the grounds of a substantial lessening of competition. The commission's role in this non-public process is to establish 'what would happen if the merger occurred' by consulting competitors (or potential competitors) of the applicants.

Having failed to secure approval for the proposed merger, the airlines then went to an adjudication process. This is a fully public process, designed to establish whether, in this case, a merger that has been disallowed on anti-competitive grounds might nevertheless be permitted on public interest grounds. During the adjudication, the airlines contended that there would be benefits to the public from the formation of a financially stronger, combined airline. Again, the ACCC found against the proposed arrangements, this time using the public consultation procedures to gauge opinion and implications. While the Federal Court reversed this decision, ultimately, the proposal did not proceed because the High Court in New Zealand blocked the merger.

A further example of the use of public consultation by the ACCC concerned the Internet-based auction web site eBay. In April 2008, eBay lodged an exclusive dealing notification with the ACCC under which it proposed to mandate the use of PayPal (a payment facility owned by eBay) for almost all transactions on <ebay.com.au>. Section 47 of the *Trade Practices Act* prohibits anti-competitive exclusive dealing that has the purpose or effect of substantially lessening competition in a relevant market. Activities such as this, however, may be allowed where it can be demonstrated that the loss can be justified in the public interest.

The ACCC's public consultation function now swung into action. In the eBay case, more than 750 submissions were received, the majority strongly critical of the PayPal requirement. Of particular interest here is that, in addition to evaluating submissions, the ACCC may organise a conference among key interested parties at the request of an interested party.

In this case, a conference was organised including eBay representatives, representatives of competing payment systems and regular users of the site. The tenor of opinion was again negative, although the deputy chair of the consultation did note that few interventions really addressed the substantive issue of market competition. As with many such consultations, most participants wanted to discuss their individual relationships with eBay, rather than the more abstract issues of interest to the commission. The commission, however, welcomed and absorbed this information in order to satisfy itself that it understood 'the whole story'. In June 2008, the ACCC issued a draft notice, giving its view that the move was likely to substantially lessen competition. eBay subsequently withdrew its notification, meaning that it no longer enjoyed immunity from prosecution under the act for the proposed arrangement with PayPal.

Managing the politics of consultation

Unlike many service delivery agencies that form part of departments of state, the ACCC has strong bulwarks against the political process. Provided it does not intrude into policy areas, it has considerable legislated independence of action. This means that the commission is able to use, and has developed, many processes over the years in order to do its work more effectively, and it may use public and non-public processes as the occasion demands. The problems of 'twin channels'—in which interests go straight to ministers—are not unknown, but the ACCC is in a good position to resist political pressure to undertake (or not to undertake) particular inquiries.

While most agencies do not have the luxury of statutory independence, the experience of the Treasury and the ACCC suggests the importance of what might be called 'the structured mandate'—that is, a clear set of objectives to be achieved through consultation and a strong reason for participation by consultees. The structured mandate is, however, only part of the story. The ACCC's watchdog role requires that it knows what is going on 'in the field'.

To this end, the ACCC maintains a number of specialised consultative bodies as a source of information on a range of consumer issues. A Consumer Consultative Committee addresses broad consumer issues; there is also a small-business advisory group and a franchising consultative panel. In addition to more general concerns, the consultative bodies are encouraged to raise issues to do with compliance—for example, in relation to pricing. In addition, the commission is often alerted to dubious practices through its complaints database and is then able to follow up through either legal action or, if more general matters are involved, by issuing (or reissuing) a consumer guide.

Managing multiple streams

One of the most difficult issues for agencies is to manage consultations involving the general public and stakeholders, particularly where stakeholders are able to lobby the minister separately from the consultation process. Treasury officials involved in the prudential review mentioned earlier stressed the importance of good communication with the minister's office and the use of informal channels to keep abreast of developments.

In the case of the ACT Planning and Land Authority, the 'multiple streams' problem arose in two ways: first, in relation to the ministerial and political dimensions of policy development; and second, in maintaining meaningful communication on a variety of highly technical issues with stakeholders and the general public.

In 2006, the ACT Government launched an ambitious plan to revamp the territory's planning and development legislation. The new act was designed to streamline the development approvals process and clarify the bases on which decisions would be made. This clarification would be achieved by defining 'tracks' that would specify the type of assessment required for particular types of development. An application assigned to the 'code' track, for example, would be automatically approved because it conformed to the relevant code—for example, the residential housing code—for land use in that area. Developments that did not conform to the code would be assessed on their merits.

The new act was voluminous and went through 52 major and minor iterations before the ACT legislature finally approved it. Many of these changes were made in response to a major consultation strategy that was coordinated by the authority. Because the new system was a major change from the old, it was essential to explain, as clearly as possible, the principles underlying the new system. At the same time, the legal form of the new system, and the draft codes through which it would be implemented, had to be progressed. As land use in the Australian Capital Territory is controlled by a leasing system, interactions between the new legislation and development rights relating to existing leases had to be carefully thought through.

The authority consulted with the industry (stakeholders) and with the community. The planners wanted to be sure that the legislation would work as intended and would be reasonably well accepted by the development industry and the public. A multi-pronged strategy was chosen: a 'roadshow' communicating with community groups and a sequence of more directed consultations with invited participants. At the same time, the authority had to ensure that lines of communication with the minister remained clear and open, as the minister engaged directly with stakeholders and made a number of key judgment calls.

The time frame for developing the legislation was restricted, so the authority began its consultation with a directions document, then an exposure draft setting out the broad architecture of the new legislation. The interest of stakeholders and the community, however, lay in the detail of the bill—what it would mean in specific situations—rather than in the broad principles of the legislation. Thus, as the consultation evolved, the authority increasingly used case studies as ways of engaging consultees. As an ACT Planning and Land Authority officer put it, 'Most people wanted to know what the rules meant for their particular situation, not the broad principles underlying the legislation. So we made a lot of use of case studies.' By illustrating what would happen in specific situations, the case studies were more effective than more abstract formulations.

Planning, as with most forms of policy, is necessarily a work in progress. Although the legislation was the end product, regulations, procedures and practices had to be established as time went on. As ACT Planning and Land Authority says, 'Consultation never ends. The conversations continue.'

Participatory decision making: natural resource management

Engagement is undoubtedly easier when there are structured relationships to work with. The Treasury case study, for example, showed the advantages, from the manager's point of view, of dealing with settled policy communities, with an agreed language of consultation. Policy communities, however, particularly in unfamiliar policy terrain, are rarely settled. Building governance—that is, the relationships that underpin and express policy—is a long-term process.

When an area is new, there is often no alternative but to experiment. John Butcher, a participant in the processes leading to the first Commonwealth–State Disability Agreement (CSDA) in 1991, recalled how early versions of the draft agreement drew strong criticism from peak bodies. In addition to meeting these objections, however, there was a need to go beyond the peak bodies, to take the agreement to the people it would be affecting most: those who would have to implement it and those who would have to live with it. As Butcher put it, there was no road-map as to how to proceed: 'We made it up as we went along.'

Over time, new forms of governance might develop. In the case of natural resource management, the need for 'fine-grained' decisions in the field has lent itself to participatory forms of interaction. The example of the east and west coast tuna fisheries shows the importance of structure (and timing) in this context, but also the capacity of experienced facilitators—in this case, public servants and consultants—to battle through ambiguity and conflict.

Governance of the two fisheries had evolved over a number of years. In the early 1990s, it was based on 'command and control'—attempts were made to conserve the resource by restricting the industry's capacity to catch fish. There was little consultation and limited conservation success. Recreational and commercial fishers were often in conflict over the terms of their respective access to the resource.

During the 1990s, clearer arrangements were established, at least as far as the commercial industry was concerned, with specified and tradable entitlements to the resource and a stronger scientific management regime, overseen by a statutory authority. Many issues remained, however, particularly relating to resource access for recreational game fishers with big boats and sophisticated equipment.

In 2002, the Commonwealth Department of Agriculture, Forests and Fisheries (DAFF) facilitated a national workshop in Coolangatta, Queensland, designed to achieve a broad consensus across all stakeholders. The government's objectives were to avoid conflict, to manage the resource sustainably and to develop mutually acceptable arrangements for resource sharing between the commercial and recreational sectors.

After an unresolved stalemate between the two sectors, a consultant (Ewan Colqhoun from Ridge Partners) was engaged to help the parties to reach specific agreements. As a result of the process, a clearer demarcation between the two levels of government was reached, stakeholders were clearly identifiable and allocations could be transferred between the two sectors. Colqhoun's role allowed the government to stand back a little from the process. As he put it, 'The role of the facilitator is to establish trust in the process.' At the same time, he could not afford to be everyone's friend. 'Both sides were annoyed with me, so I knew I must be getting it right.'

This was a hard-edged process, in which claims for attention had to be backed up with facts and data. This tended to disadvantage the recreational fishing industry, which had not previously quantified its activities to any great degree, but to be in the process at all, the industry had to conform to its requirements. Expectations of influence had to be matched by information. 'Where are your data? If you want to be listened to, you must have data.'

As the process unfolded, discussion literally edged to a compromise. Finer-scale data were generated. Specific zones of conflict, between recreational and commercial fishers, were identified. As a result of the participatory process, there was better analysis of the data and a more rigorous definition of total biological load—that is, the extent to which the fishery was to be exploited. Social, biological and economic considerations were included in the analysis.

The facilitator's role was that of honest information broker. Transparency was essential as, without trust, little could be achieved. As information accreted, the facilitator had to ensure that it was disseminated, so that parties understood the exact positions of others. Motivation for the consultation was strong, based on a shared desire to secure fishery access rights, sustain the marine environment and to build data and management capacity.

In this type of consultation, language and numbers are of equal importance. Data are key—they must be relevant, accurate and timely. While the ultimate policy advice remained with the department (and the final decisions with the minister), the facilitator allowed the department to maintain (or reduce) its distance from the negotiators. The skills required of the facilitator included technical knowledge, the ability to chair sessions, attention to detail and being firm on principles, even when this courted unpopularity. As DAFF officer Dr Liz Foster put it, 'In theory, it's as easy as carving up a pie, except that the size of the pie is unknown, the sizes of the pieces are unknown, and there are many managers of the same pie. Perceptions, as well as realities, must be managed.'

Water policy provides further examples of evolving governance. The field is immensely complex in Australia, involving multiple levels of governance (local, regional, state and national) and a plethora of public agencies and organised interests, all interacting with each other to produce recurrent and, with the advent of seemingly endless drought, chronic environmental problems. The 'community' component of this complex tapestry comprises catchment management authorities, established under state legislation and bringing together representatives from government, the community and industry.

For more than 20 years, catchment management authorities formed part of the intricate tapestry of Australian environmental federalism. These were highly participatory bodies, established by the states, to align decision making with ecological and community boundaries. Not surprisingly, many catchment management authorities had an uneasy relationship with the governments that had given rise to them and, more particularly, with the long-established water-management departments that exercised executive power. The NSW State Government disbanded the Hawkesbury-Nepean Trust, for example, in 2001 and its powers were absorbed back into the Department of Land and Water Conservation.

In 2006–07, residents of Queensland's Mary River Valley, who, as participants in a catchment management group, had worked hard on a water management plan for many years, found that the state government had decreed that a new dam was to be built on the river in the heart of their valley, completely overturning community-oriented planning and interests. In these cases, the politics of growth and the interests of existing bureaucracies worked against participatory governance.

The takeover of water management powers by the Federal Government in 2007–08 and the formation of a National Water Commission allowed the states to focus on the implementation of change. Implementation involved consultation and participation: the terms of the National Water Initiative required state governments to consult communities and to report on their progress. In New South Wales, for example, catchment management authorities were involved in consultations about the classification of the water-sharing rules for each of 43 water-sharing plans (NSW 2006). In every state, catchment management authorities are invoked as the mechanism for consultation, although in most instances, existing agencies take the lead role.

Once a basis for action has been established, consultation gives way to decision making. As with the tuna fisheries example discussed earlier, participatory processes have become more prominent as managers have battled to bring together the data and the action needed to produce outcomes. Irrigators in south-eastern South Australia have, through participatory processes, provided data for the conversion of area-based licences to volumetric water licences (Carruthers et al. 2006).

Similar processes were used to establish a water-pricing mechanism after the damming of Queensland's Burnett River. The *Queensland Water Act 2000* required a water-pricing pathway for the next 10 years. A consultation was organised to provide data for the construction of a demand/price function, facilitated by a consultant. Once again, while the final ratification of the water-sharing plan rested with the minister, the consultative process—perhaps we might call it 'participatory consultation'—enabled decisions to be mapped with a precise understanding of their real effects on stakeholders.

These consultations have a decision-making and a learning function. As consultant Colquhoun describes it, farmers often do not understand their business dynamics or the impact of particular issues. If the process succeeds, however, as Carruthers et al. (2006:1) put it, 'broad community involvement in data collection and decision making promotes shared ownership of outcomes'. This type of consultation would appear to have many other applications—for example, in modelling the effects on greenhouse-gas emitters of particular emissions-reductions scenarios. It would also appear to have considerable applicability to at least some of the 'retrenchment' scenarios outlined later in this chapter.

Using the right language for engagement

There is a need to create a language *of* engagement and a language *for* engagement. The way we see policy has a strong bearing on the types of language that are considered appropriate. If we see policy solely in terms of rational inquiry and report, we miss the felt sense of engagement, the stories that are told to illuminate or justify positions.

The choice of target group reflects a certain understanding as to what the consultation is about and what it can do. As one commentator at our forum put it, 'Who you talk to determines the meaning.' The need to have data in order to have a seat at the table can legitimate the consultation from a rational perspective, but it creates a sense of exclusion. On the other hand, genuine efforts to present technical information in clearly argued ways might enlarge the consultation space, as the 2008 Garnaut reports on emissions trading showed.

Scientific information poses particular problems. Scientists do not deal in certainties and sometimes not even in probabilities. Managers and policy makers, however, need information on which they can act. Communities need technical information 'translated' into terms they can understand. This is particularly important in consulting about water-quality standards. What does 'so many parts per million' of a specified pollutant in a much-loved river mean in human terms? Can you swim in the water?

As we saw in the case of the ACT Planning and Land Authority, the key to successful engagement proved to be the use of case studies that addressed the question 'What will the change mean for me?'. Preparation of this type of material, however, is expensive and time consuming. Members of the public who wish to make representations about specific development applications must wrestle with the opacities of planning language and conventions, rather than enjoying the convenience of three-dimensional representations of planned change (although this might change with the advent of new software for modelling building information). The way information is presented is as political as the consultation itself.

Consultation as learning: the role of parliamentary committees

Political necessity, time and resources often circumscribe executive-initiated inquiries. Parliamentary inquiries do not have these same constraints. They get 'out and about' to an extraordinary degree. As the secretary to an inquiry into an environmental issue put it, 'It was only when we actually got to the area that the committee began to understand what the community was talking about.'

Academic Ian Holland points out that parliamentary inquiries constitute an opportunity for politicians to 'de-role' (act outside their customary party-political roles) and to learn in an open way from those contributing. [2] A good secretariat can tap into a wide range of invited opinion. The committee can talk 'in real time' to participants in ways that are intimate while also being public. As Annette Ellis, chair of a House of Representatives social policy committee, put it,

'[H]earing the stories of carers, sitting around the table with them, created a really powerful impression on us all.'[3]

Public servants, much more constrained in how they talk to the public, could make more use of parliamentary sources of information. At the same time, public servants might find parliamentary processes immensely frustrating. As servants of the Executive, it is not their role to suggest questions to the politicians. 'Often,' said one senior officer, 'valuable time is wasted because the Parliament does not know the right questions to ask.'

Speaking to government, speaking to constituents

Agenda setting requires the delineation of an issue in a way that will fit with the priorities of government. Organisations that wish to lobby government on behalf of a widely dispersed membership base need to find good issues to highlight and good ways of using the resources of members to attract government's attention.

In 2007, the Australian Local Government Association (ALGA), frustrated by the lack of attention given to local government issues, decided to try something new. The association, a peak body with a membership consisting of state associations, developed an 'ideas register' to bring the run-down state of community infrastructure to the attention of the Federal Government. The register would not only record words, it would use photographic evidence ('pictures') to make its point.

The association knew, however, that, in the hard-edged world of government, it needed to communicate using a number of modes. In 2006, ALGA had commissioned a study by consultants into the financial sustainability of local government. The study recommended the establishment of a 'community infrastructure initiative' that would assist councils to renew aged and failing community infrastructure such as swimming pools, community halls and libraries.

In March 2007, the ideas register was launched via the ALGA web site. The objective of the register was to give councils and private citizens the opportunity to identify specific examples of local community infrastructure that would benefit from such an initiative. By November 2007, more than 1000 ideas—and associated photographs—had been lodged on the register. The response from local communities and local government was overwhelming. Most submissions (28 per cent) related to run-down facilities.

The funds were not, however, immediately forthcoming. The incoming Rudd Labor Government implemented a review into the previous government's Regional Partnerships Program, through the House of Representatives' Standing Committee on Infrastructure, Transport, Regional Development and Local Government. ALGA made a submission to this inquiry, using material from the ideas register.

The agenda might have been influenced, but securing real funding would be another matter. Local government's ability to influence the Federal Government directly had, perhaps ironically, to be channelled through an examination of the previous government's program (which had favoured relatively few applications for assistance from local government).

Managing expectations

Managing expectations in situations of power imbalance and ambiguity is, obviously, a difficult thing to do. Explaining to consultees the politics of a particular situation is not normally the job of public servants. Even if it were, political processes are complex and there is much that cannot readily be predicted. Having some sense of what community expectations really are, and addressing them up front, is useful.

One of the criticisms of community consultation voiced most frequently by those consulted is that no notice is taken of the views expressed. There might be many reasons why decisions do not reflect community views, but in many cases, community disappointment is as much about the process as the outcome. Clearly, where this is the case, there has been a failure by those running the consultation to explain to those consulted why their views are being sought and what difference they might make to the final outcome.

Researchers report many instances where consultation has had little or no impact on the structures and processes it was, ostensibly, meant to effect. In 2005, Mark Walters documented the lack of influence of the Police Accountability Community Teams that were meant to make NSW policing more responsive to the needs of communities. With no leadership 'from the top', control rested solely in the hands of police who chose how much or how little effect the meetings with the community would have on community policing. Where police representatives reported back on specific issues raised by the team, resident participation and interest remained strong. Where there was little interest, the meetings dwindled away (Walters 2005).

Economic interests often have overwhelming power. Susan Oakley (2007) reported on plans to revitalise the Port Adelaide waterfront that stressed high-density, up-market development designed to bring a designated return on investment. Residents who participated in consultation sessions felt they were being pressured to endorse a particular kind of 're-imagined' waterfront, one that would exacerbate differences between those living in the redeveloped area and others (Oakley 2007).

This kind of pre-existing bias has been documented across a range of fields, such as efforts to find sites for nuclear waste (Holland 2002). It is not, however, only members of the public who find themselves on the outer. On occasion, stakeholders have found themselves subject to a 'Clayton's' consultation. In the mid-1990s, although they were ostensibly consulted, juvenile justice practitioners in Queensland found themselves sidelined by the Goss Government's desire to show itself to be 'tough on crime' for political reasons (Hill and Roughley 1997).

On occasion, consultation has underlined the extent of community frustration with consultation itself. As far back as 1994, community-controlled health organisations in the Northern Territory were telling the then Federal Labor Government how tired they were of being consulted, their weariness with the many reports that had been produced 'and the failure of this to come back to Aboriginal people, with there being no demonstrable benefits to health resulting from this activity to date' (Department of Health and Aging 1995).

The continuing battle between pro-development state governments and local communities, the latter often championed by local government, washes through many institutional structures. Prospects might be better when consultation is itself the result of hard-fought battles. Local residents had an important role to play in the retention in public hands of Callan Park, the site of a mental health facility occupying 61 hectares of prime land in Sydney. Because of determined activism by the community, detailed consultations were held about the development of public plans for the site, leading to the granting to Leichhardt Council of a 99-year lease over 40 hectares of the site (Sydney Harbour Foreshore Authority 2008; Parker 2008).

What do communities expect of consultation processes? While few practitioner-based evaluations of consultations are available, we do have some evidence from the environmental field. In 1997–98, the NSW Environment Protection Authority (NSW EPA) conducted an interim evaluation of its community consultation on environmental flows and water quality. The original program was designed 'to give a statewide perspective on what people participating in the consultation program thought of the health of their river systems, the values they place on their waterways, and the environmental issues they identified as priority concerns' (Environment Protection Authority of New South Wales 1998).

The format of the consultation was an ambitious one, with some deliberative elements, although this was not a term the NSW EPA used. A discussion paper was prepared and community meetings organised in 44 places. More than 4000 people attended the meetings, at which facilitated discussions on water quality were held. Subsequently, more than 800 written submissions were made to the NSW EPA, of which more than 600 were from individuals. When the draft interim guidelines on water quality were published, further community input was obtained and substantial changes made as a result. The draft guidelines were then submitted to the government.

When the NSW EPA asked those involved what they thought of the process, many people responded in ways that suggested impatience with or scepticism about the purpose of the consultation. There was a cynical element: many people thought that the NSW Government had already made up its mind and the consultation was for show only. Others said that the consultation was not necessary and that action, rather than further discussion, was required.

Clearly, it is important for regulators in these situations not to allow inflated expectations of the engagement process to emerge. In 2001, the EPA in Western Australia conducted a public consultation on the environmental values of Perth's coastal waters. The WA EPA's discussion document, referring to earlier consultations, was at pains to point out that holistic options for environmental management were not available (Government of Western Australia, n.d.). Important activities such as fishing continued to be regulated by other agencies. In reflecting on this history in a public way, the agency was communicating to communities what the management framework could (and could not) do. Such realism might not excite communities and might diminish participation in the exercise, but this might be a reasonable price to pay for not overloading the process.

Summing up

The case studies suggest that Australian public managers are not often in a situation in which they are able to choose their engagement strategy. The mandate and powers of their agency shape purpose and practice. Within these parameters, however, many choices are made—and outside them, an appreciation of the contending forces that might be at work suggests pathways of influence and, on occasion, avoidance.

Strategies that work make use of public and non-public aspects of consultation, they manage expectations by communicating clearly and establishing trust and they emphasise 'getting out there' into the field. Engagement is about understanding where people are coming from and making sure they know which of their concerns might (or might not) be affected as a result of their participation.

Endnotes

[1] My thanks to Andre Moore (Treasury), Hank Spier (consultant), Nigel Ridgway and Darrell Channing (ACCC), Ewan Colquhoun (Ridge Partners), Amanda Lynch (ALGA), David Dunstan (ACTPLA), Ian Holland (Department of the Senate), Llewellyn Reinders (ACTCOSS), Mark de Weerd (DEEWR), John Butcher (ANZSOG) and Kate Hay (Centrelink) for providing case studies in Chapters 4 and 5. I have contributed the structuring and broader interpretation of the case studies.

[2] Ian Holland, speaking at the Dilemmas of Engagement Consultation Forum, 22 August 2008.

[3] Annette Ellis MP, speaking at World Mental Health Day Function, Canberra, 10 October 2008.

5. Improving consultation practice

In this chapter, I consider problematic applications of consultation. These are the instances in which consultation seems to create more difficulties than it resolves or in which it is politically difficult to undertake consultation in the first place. The emphasis throughout is on practical remedies. The first section of the chapter discusses consultation from the viewpoint of community groups, drawing on practical examples of the kinds of behaviours that, while perfectly reasonable from a public management point of view, cause confusion and loss of trust among consultees. The second section discusses a number of cases in which consultation has not produced the benefits expected of it, and asks how the process could have been better handled.

Consultation and the seven bureaucratic sins

'The community' often enrages or disappoints governments, especially when it does not come up with the answer that the experts want. Equally, however, government has a maddening effect on communities. Most public servants have little idea how difficult it is for communities to understand the bureaucratic process. From the community's perspective, problems are seamless. From government's perspective, problems are defined by the functional arrangements that have been put in place for dealing with them.

A representative of a prominent peak body provided the following insights into 'the seven bureaucratic sins' and the effects these practices have on the community and some of the ways in which public servants can address the problems (see figure 5.1 below). [1]

Dealing with the silos

Many of the sins of bureaucracy result from a lack of communication between and within agencies: the tendency for public servants to view the world from the perspective of the 'silo', or functional hierarchy, to which they belong. When it comes to engaging with communities more directly, whether the objective is to solve problems or to produce outcomes, the effects of the silos become even more problematic. Two case studies—the Murdi Paaki COAG field trial and Centrelink's Murray-Darling Basin initiative—show what can be done when agencies are prepared to think and to work more flexibly.

Table 5.1 The seven bureaucratic sins of consultation

1. 'You're off the topic'	Many points that are raised in consultations are not relevant to the designated topic and/or participants have not fully read the consultation documents. There is a tendency to ignore or sideline concerns that are not relevant to the matter in hand.	Suggested remedy: even if it's off the topic, at least pass the point on to the person whose responsibility it is.
2. 'That's not our job'	The consultees have read all the documents, but their particular concern falls between several agencies—in other words, no-one is dealing with it.	Remedy: try to pass the information to the agency that should take it up or at least suggest that the person writes to the minister about it, and suggest which minister they should approach.
3. 'Consulting on motherhood statements'	The consultation never gets near anything controversial or even concrete. The propositions put forward cannot be disagreed with, but the same questions have been canvassed previously, often many times over. Consultation fatigue quickly sets in when this happens.	Remedy: check to see what others have done. If there is a real need to proceed, have something specific to talk to the community about. If you are consulting on something broad, such as a health strategy, try to give people some sense of what particular elements might mean for them.
4. 'You can't come in here'	The desire for control sometimes results in consultations that are not open to groups whose views are not sought or whose participation is not welcome. At times, there are really difficult scenes when people are physically prevented from coming into the room.	Remedy: if you can't handle the heat, don't hold the consultation.
5. 'Contrived support'	Agencies often misrepresent the true outcomes of consultation. They say, 'We've consulted on this', giving the impression that their view enjoys widespread support. Or they consult using leading questions that push people's views in certain directions.	Remedy: report fully on what you have found, even if it is negative.

6. 'The black hole'	Lots of issues come up through the consultation, only to disappear into the black hole of the bureaucracy. Those who participated in the process hear nothing until an announcement is made, but often there is no tangible outcome at all.	Remedy: agencies should produce a consultation report that conveys the comments that were made. Privacy concerns should be dealt with by asking permission for names to be used.
7. 'The left hand and the right hand'	Decisions are made (often in a budgetary context) that affect a number of programs, leaving 'unconsulted' community organisations with contracts to deliver these programs. The collective impacts on the organisations concerned can be quite heavy. A variation on this theme occurs when a decision in one department impacts directly on the ability of a community organisation, contracted to another, to deliver a program.	Remedy: better coordination mechanisms are needed, particularly where community organisations are delivering programs to a number of different agencies. Compacts between government and the community sector should make specific mention of these kinds of issues.

Murdi Paaki

Murdi Paaki is a region of western New South Wales that takes in 16 Indigenous communities including those of Bourke, Broken Hill and Brewarrina. In 2003, an agreement was signed between the Murdi Paaki Regional Council and the Commonwealth Department of Education, Science and Training (DEST) to implement an innovative field trial designed to improve outcomes in health, education and economic development.

The field trial was sponsored by COAG and was based on a philosophy of proactive partnership between Indigenous communities, state and Commonwealth departments and non-governmental organisations (NGOs). The Indigenous communities wanted action across a range of issues, but were tired of years of well-intentioned government intervention that achieved few lasting results. The task of the public servants was to establish ways of working with the communities that would develop trust and deliver real outcomes.

Shared responsibility was one of the underlying principles of the trial. Twenty-nine shared-responsibility agreements were signed, forming a basis for ownership of the changes that were implemented. The governance structures chosen reflected a new way of thinking, one that aligned bureaucratic ways of working more closely with those of the local people. For example, the local people's preference was for loose working groups that were as representative as possible of particular communities. In order to work with these communities, the public service departments had to work through local representatives of the departments involved.

These local representatives formed action teams that worked closely with community groups and the regional council to identify specific actions that needed to be pursued (Jarvie 2008). This activity was backed up by, and oriented towards, measurable improvements in key indicators, such as school attendance and literacy. As Sam Jeffries (2008), chair of the Murdi Paaki Regional Council put it, '[W]e concentrated on the results, rather than competing for the dollars to achieve the results.'

What was being established here? In the technical sense, we might see a mode of governance that aligned resources with change. When we look deeper, we see that the people themselves determined the priorities and the government agencies worked at linking that way of thinking with their need for performance indicators. Administration was thereby personalised. Information flowed from the ground upwards.

Information also had to flow across departmental boundaries. In some ways, this was the greatest challenge of all. Departments that were accustomed to working in particular modes, and ignoring (or fighting) others, had to shed their habitual ways of working. For many, this proved very difficult. As Mark de Weerd, leader of the action team, puts it, when you have a sympathetic manager, you can achieve anything. Governments were prepared, in this case, to learn from communities and to allow the communities to engage them, rather than the other way around.

Structures and processes, however, were important, as were the principles governing communication. Form followed function. One of the most successful subgroups was set up to deal with employment, education and training. This subgroup brought together local representatives of some 10 government departments, representatives from the regional assembly and five NGOs. The main resources were people and the capacity they represented. When money was needed for particular purposes, however—such as building a swimming pool in Brewarrina—it was speedily found.

What is remarkable about Murdi Paaki is the fact that public servants on the ground were supported in developing engagement. With a political warrant from COAG, a high-level group had the authority that was needed. In turn, this group gave members of the action teams the flexibility they needed. If things needed to be done differently, the support was there. If more time was needed, it was given. Even so, some agencies were not able to suspend habitual ways of working in order to meet communities' needs. Others were. Often, this meant a willingness to adapt what could be done, within an agency's budget and framework, to the need. For example, DEST was able to assist in work on the Collarenebri Cemetery by creating a training position to get the job done.

Centrelink's Murray-Darling Basin Project

In April 2007, there was growing concern about the social impacts of the devastating drought that was afflicting the Murray-Darling Basin. The May 2007 Budget appropriated $10 million to Centrelink as part of a special project to provide additional support to drought-affected communities, particularly communities of irrigators who were facing zero water allocations from July 2007. The project presented Centrelink with the challenge of identifying and working with a large number of stakeholders—internal and external—and establishing a community engagement model that was helpful, without heightening people's concerns.

A Service Delivery Coordination Unit, based in Griffith, New South Wales, was established to coordinate a broad range of government programs in the area. The inspiration for the unit came from the success of the 'quick-response' teams that provided practical help in the aftermath of Cyclone Larry in Queensland. In addition, the availability of specific assistance, in the form of a new Irrigation Management Grant, was an important catalyst in establishing contact with the many stakeholders involved.

The money, while important, was, however, only part of the picture. Having the flexibility to provide practical 'linking' services was also vital. In this context, the staffing of the unit proved crucial to the success of the initiative. 'We didn't have a "budget" as such, for what we were doing,' says Kate Hay, national manager of Centrelink Rural. 'What we did have were people. When community groups asked for help, sending them the right person at the right time could open doors, and help make things happen.'

The Centrelink and Murdi Paaki stories show what can be done when capacity is placed at the service of need. There are, however, particular requirements for this type of engagement to be successful. The Murdi Paaki field trial showed agencies working with communities to make decisions about what they would do. The Centrelink Murray-Darling Basin Unit had no preset agenda, but offered guidance where it was needed. In both cases, the lead agency had to be prepared to use its programs and its people flexibly. The lead agency had to possess the resources and the reach to make a difference, although the real actions taken were often on quite a small scale. Although high-level support was required for these initiatives, the risks involved in really doing things—that is, responding to situations on the ground—proved to be small.

Consultation when the news is bad

> People are all in favour of consultation, but only when the results go their way.
>
> (Former senior public servant, Federal Department of Education, speaking in 2008)

When governments are handing out benefits, they run relatively few short-term risks if they do not consult, or consult poorly. Benefits given to one group might antagonise others, but are unlikely to cause major political upheavals. The story is a different one when governments have to manage retractions, closures and retrenchments or even changes, which, if badly managed, can lead to considerable antagonism.

Some of the most intractable problems arise when there is a need to get consultees onside, but the fate that is in store for them is unattractive. Not surprisingly, these situations are often mishandled. Governments do not trumpet their 'bad news' consultations, so there is not much public soul-searching about these episodes. Precisely because of the mistrust that is generated, however, and the dismay of many activists' and citizens' groups, there are many instances on the political record. Here, we look at three instances of this problem and ask how it might have been done better.

The Traveston Crossing Dam

In July 2006, at the height of the 2000–07 drought, the Queensland Government announced its plan to build a dam on the Mary River, north of Brisbane. The decision to dam the river was taken after a 'desk-top review' of possible dam sites compiled by consultants GHD (Senate Standing Committee on Rural and Regional Affairs and Transport 2007). There had been no prior consultation with local people, despite the existence of a well-established catchment management authority for the region.

There were fiery meetings in the Mary River Valley about the plan. Not only would the dam flood many hectares of prime agricultural land, including one of the state's largest dairy farms, even with mitigating action, the dam would adversely affect the habitats of a number of endangered species, including the Mary River turtle and the Mary River cod. When the state-level environmental impact assessment (EIA) process was opened, more than 16 000 submissions were received.

Environmental impact assessment is a broad-ranging process that is public and consultation based. In these cases, consultation is mandated, but structured in ways that 'mobilise bias' towards development. As I put it in an article on the dam (Stewart 2008b), '[T]he process is carefully stage-managed. And as activists everywhere have discovered, "they" (the authorities) have everything—time, power, expertise and money—on their side.'

Where governments are themselves proponents of change, consultation has a particularly hollow ring. In the Mary River case, the Queensland Coordinator-General was charged with the responsibility for determining the response to the state-based EIA process, but the proponents of the dam, Queensland Water Infrastructure (QWI), were themselves wholly owned by the Queensland Government and involved in a number of ways in the project. During 2007, QWA bought many properties in the valley. Locals sold because of the uncertainty of their future.

The Commonwealth, under the terms of the *Environmental Planning and Biodiversity Conservation Act*, must also be involved and the Federal Minister for the Environment has the final say as to whether the project is to proceed or not. Public servants advising the minister clearly have a pivotal role to play, but while lobbying continues, consultation does not. Only the Senate, through its Standing Committee on Rural and Regional Affairs and Transport, consulted widely—and even then it brought down a non-committal report.

How could this process have been better managed?

EIAs have been heavily criticised for their failure to deal, fully and openly, with community objections to development. One model is for the State itself—so often ranged against the interests of concerned citizens—to take its part in legal proceedings. In Sweden, the State may play this role by representing citizens in environment courts used to determine permits for large installations. [2]

Whether or not courts are involved, consultative balance would seem to require the construction of new arenas to enable community views to be heard. In the case of the Mary River, the problem arose because the Queensland Government panicked in the face of unprecedented drought and did not give itself sufficient time to find out the true political (and ecological) parameters of the dam site its consultants had suggested. More research before the EIA process was even invoked would have facilitated more accurate risk assessment.

School closures in the Australian Capital Territory

The ACT *Education Act 2004* requires communities to be consulted when closures of government schools are contemplated. Before closing or amalgamating a school, the minister is required to:

(a) have regard to the educational, financial and social impact on students at the school, the students' families and the general school community; and

> (b) ensure that school communities affected by the closure or amalgamation have been adequately consulted during a period of at least 6 months. (s. 20, clause 5)

The act further states that 'consultation should be open and transparent' and 'should lead to sustainable decisions by involving effective community engagement'. To enable effective consultation to take place, relevant information should be provided in 'a timely and accessible way'.

These aspirations might have been achievable where one or two schools were concerned. They became almost impossible to implement in circumstances in which multiple school closures were on the agenda. In May 2006, the ACT Government, believing that it was faced with a major budget deficit, announced plans to close 39 schools and preschools. Many of these schools had low enrolments and had been under-enrolled for a number of years. Demographic change, as families aged and the number of school-age children fell, was one precipitating factor. There had also been a drift from government to non-government education.

Why such a large number of schools and preschools? There was some speculation that the government was, in effect, making an ambit claim and was prepared from the outset to concede on some closures (in the final analysis, 24 schools and preschools were closed). If this was so, it is hard to see what 'consultation' was designed to achieve, unless the government believed that in setting community against community, it was shoring up support in the areas surrounding the 'saved' schools.

Not surprisingly, the climate of consultation became highly charged, as communities organised to defend their schools. It soon became apparent that the government had not researched the case for closure in great detail in each instance. Under vigorous questioning from community representatives, public servants from the Department of Education, charged with presenting rationales for the closures, often seemed under-prepared. What was ostensibly a consultation was, in reality, a multilateral negotiation, with citizens defining and redefining the case for keeping their school open, in the light of any feedback they received.

The government tried valiantly to package its final decision as a major breakthrough for government schooling. New schools catering for preschool to year 10 would be built, embodying (so it was claimed) the latest educational principles. The territory's budgetary outcome, however, was more favourable than expected, adding to community cynicism that a prearranged agenda had been imposed on them.

Having finally made its decision, the government was not about to backtrack, even when, in 2007, it found that more money was available than previously thought. In 2008, however, with an election approaching, the government realised it had to mend bridges with the community, particularly in relation to the fate of the former school sites. It was widely expected that the government, committed to expanding the supply of housing in the territory, would move quickly to sell off the sites, many of which were in prime residential locations close to shops.

Reacting to criticism that it had not consulted in good faith previously, the government now undertook a further two rounds of consultations, both facilitated by firms of consultants. The first was designed to determine community sentiment about the future of the former school sites. The response was unequivocal: the community was strongly opposed to any sell off and wanted the schools preserved for community use. Realising it had set the parameters too broadly, the government now commissioned a further, more tightly defined consultation designed to elicit support for partial use of a number of the sites for multi-unit housing. It was widely claimed that the government would keep consulting the community until the community told it what it wanted to hear.

How could this process have been better managed?

The government failed to think strategically about the future and its public servants clearly failed to alert it to the dangers it was running. A more considered process—one that tapped community sentiment while presenting, as clearly as possible, the budgetary facts—might have averted the drawn out confrontation that resulted. It might also have prevented the government from being portrayed by its opponents as remote and out of touch.

In an effort to improve its consultative credentials, the government put out a discussion paper that promised to 'put citizens at the centre of policy development' (Stanhope 2008). The paper recommended a number of reforms, including enhanced electronic engagement of citizens and improved information dissemination by the government.

Local government amalgamations in Queensland

In 2007, the then Queensland Premier, Peter Beattie, announced that local governments would be amalgamated. The number of councils would be reduced by more than half, from 156 to 72, and more than 700 councillors would lose their jobs. The reasons behind the change seemed compelling: population growth, environmental stress and planning problems were creating problems that local governments, many of them fragmented and small, were ill equipped to handle. The government was particularly concerned about south-east Queensland, where the presence of 18 local councils made the coordination of planning very difficult.

In this case, a consultative process undertaken under the auspices of a Local Government Reform Commission, and with the active involvement of the

Queensland Local Government Association (LGA), had been in train for some time. An impatient treasurer, however, short-circuited the process, clearly with the idea that more development-compliant, as well as more efficient, entities would result.

If the government had hoped that more development-compliant councils would result, it was disappointed in at least some instances. The amalgamated Sunshine Coast Council elected as mayor the Mayor of Noosa, one council that had tried to prevent Gold Coast-style high-rise development.

Not surprisingly, the government had poisoned its relations with the local government sector. As commentator Scott Prasser (2007) observed, from 1998, when Premier Beattie first came to power,

> collaboration and co-operation with local government was the order of the day as shown by the regular renewal of a memorandum of understanding between the Queensland Government and the Local Government Association of Queensland (LGAQ) and state government support for the LGAQ's *Size, Shape and Sustainability* (SSS) review into the viability of local government and voluntary amalgamation. (Prasser 2007)

The government's decision to end the discussion, and impose an external review, was, not surprisingly, viewed as a betrayal of trust. As Councillor Paul Bell put it:

> Why kill the *Size, Shape, and Sustainability*? Why not confide in local government if the state was unhappy with progress…Why the deceitful charade over the first three months of the year (i.e. 2007). The LGAQ was deceived, so were mayors and council CEOs, even the Independent Review Facilitators (of the SSS process) right up to the very last day. (Quoted in Prasser 2007)

What went wrong here? As with the school closures in the Australian Capital Territory, what we appear to be seeing is a consultation process that has to do double duty as a negotiation process. There seems little doubt that a consensual result of the *SSS* review would not have produced the swinging cuts that the final review effected. Again, had the government put its real plan on the table, and presumably been forced to discuss its underlying political agenda, the final result would have been some kind of compromise.

How could this process have been better managed?

Inevitably, the answers to intergovernmental questions are more political than administrative. If governments are punished at the polls for riding roughshod over community opinion, they will quickly learn to adopt a more pragmatic approach. For reforming governments, the stakes are particularly high. In

Victoria, the Kennett Government initially tried to encourage voluntary amalgamations among councils, but later abandoned this approach and determined the boundaries without consultation.

Over time, however, the government's very power to impose its model of local government produced a climate of antagonism so pronounced that voters punished the government by voting in a more gently reformist Labor regime under Steve Bracks.

For public servants, the lessons could be that where negotiation is required, a negotiation (rather than a consultation) stance should be adopted and the emphasis placed on the clarification and resolution of differences, rather than on the public airing of issues. The term 'review', which implies consultation rather than negotiation, can obscure rather than illuminate this distinction.

Rural and Remote Area Health Services in Western Australia

Consultation occurs frequently in relation to health service provision at the local level. The evaluative literature, however, in the words of Durey and Lockhart (2004:97), 'abounds with examples of the disparity between institutional rhetoric and the reality of practice when it comes to health programs that aim to put the community first'.

An illustrative case study shows the problems that can arise when there is a disjunction between the managerial/professional agendas and those of local communities. The context is that of the introduction of a Multipurpose Health Service (MPS) in rural Western Australia. [3] The parameters will be familiar to many readers. During the 1990s, the Commonwealth and state governments were concerned that rural health services were being delivered in a manner that was not only inefficient (because of the duplication of many services), but was failing to keep pace with the changing needs of communities. Budgetary stringency, as well as a genuine need for change, had created a window of opportunity for far-reaching reform.

An MPS, the professionals were convinced, filled the bill. They were keen to implement the program across the state. Community consultation was necessary, according to the Health Department of Western Australia, to ensure that all participants were fully informed and endorsed each step of the process towards the goal. The consultations, however, did not go to plan. Two WA towns, Diamond Head and Wongabeena (both names are pseudonyms), were chosen for an evaluation of the issues involved.

For the professionals, the objectives of the MPS were clear. They were to centralise control of the administration of health services in the two towns and to provide a common pool of funding that would then be used to provide services in line with community needs.

As interpreted by the community, these objectives meant just one thing: reductions in existing services. It was not surprising, then, that as the consultation developed, the atmosphere became more and more heated. Residents of Wongabeena feared that their hospital would be lost or downgraded and that services would shift to the more rapidly growing, tourist-based town of Diamond Head. For their part, Diamond Head residents were concerned that directives from health department bureaucrats would overwhelm their nursing service.

This was not at all the consultative agenda that those in charge had mapped out. Health department public servants and professionals in the field had envisaged an orderly process of information gathering to determine community needs. To this end, a consultative committee had been formed, comprising broad-based input from the community at large, and allowing for as diverse a range of participants as possible.

An initial attempt to survey residents produced a modest response: 17 per cent of the surveys sent out were returned. Efforts to obtain written input failed dismally. Town meetings were subsequently set up and these were well attended. By this time, alarm bells were ringing, not just in the community, but among stakeholders (hospital committee members, GPs and nurses).

While the professionals believed the community had been consulted, the community and stakeholders felt that they had not been consulted at all, because the key issues (for them) had not been aired. As one GP put it, 'It was the traditional government approach. We know what is good for you. We had to push ourselves forward to have our say' (Durey and Lockhart 2004:103).

How could the process have been better managed?

Clearly, the professionals should have found better ways of explaining their intentions to the community. They might reply that no such better way existed. As we noted earlier, the more sensitive the issue, the more difficult it is for governments to consult, without the issue spinning out of control. On the other hand, the more controversial the issue, the more important it is that affected communities should be consulted. There often seems to be an inverse correlation between the need for consultation and the likelihood that it will occur.

In these kinds of situations, governments might feel they are damned if they do and damned if they don't. The goal, however, need not necessarily be to secure 'buy-in' to decisions that are going to prove unpopular. Citizens appreciate they might not always get what they want, but they are less likely to feel aggrieved if they believe that they have, at least, been heard.

'We arranged a consultation and no-one came'

Many participatory exercises fail to get off the ground because they do not provide adequate incentives for citizens to become involved. Irvine and

Stansbury's analysis of Papillion Creek near urban Omaha, Nebraska is a case in point. They ran a consultation and no-one came, because citizens were not sufficiently dissatisfied with the status quo to turn up (Irvine and Stansbury 2004).

Similarly, consulting on 'motherhood' statements, particularly when they are the same 'motherhood statements' presented over and over again, is unlikely to generate much community interest. One of the abiding dilemmas of consultation is that communities are least likely to miss consultation when the system is working well. It is when material change is on the agenda that people most want to know. Then, however, governments are least inclined to tell.

Some personal experience goes to this point. I remember agreeing, as the vice-president of a community group, to chair a consultative meeting about a new housing development. Everyone was there: the public servants from the development authority, the engineers, architects and landscape designers from the firm that would build the development—everyone, in fact, except the public. There was one chap who showed up to everything, because he had a passion for talking about the problems of solar orientation, and there were a couple of other people who seemed to have wandered in. There were lengthy presentations from the experts but, apart from the solar orientation chap, no questions.

In the course of the evening, I learned that the development in question would, in due course, be flanked by two high-rise office blocks. When I attempted to ask about these, however, I was told that they had nothing to do with the estate development and would, in any case, be the subject of separate development applications. Someone asked about the large concrete stormwater drains that ran past the site—there had been some talk about 'softening' these—but there was no information forthcoming here either. Another inquiry, involving another part of the bureaucracy, was supposed to be dealing with this. All fair enough, but why hold the consultation in the first place? The answer was that as a preliminary assessment for a new estate development, the proponent was required to tick the box on public consultation. There was, however, nothing particularly controversial about the new estate to talk about.

On another occasion, as a new mother, I attended a session on maternal services in the Australian Capital Territory. This was, literally, a 'motherhood' consultation. There had been announcements about the sessions in baby health clinics, but again, hardly anyone turned up. There were plenty of issues to interest new mothers: the lack of a birthing centre in the local hospital was a continuing concern. The department, however, already knew about this problem, because the community had told it about it. Setting up a very general consultation about 'services', and pursuing it through an open meeting, was doomed to fail.

How could the process have been better managed?

Attracting people to meetings means consulting on issues that are of importance to them and recognising that consultation has costs as well as benefits. Some of these costs can be difficult to measure, particularly when they fall on citizens and community organisations. For community groups, the opportunity costs of involvement in traditional advisory or consultative bodies can be far greater than the travel allowances and sitting fees that usually accompany them.

Benefits can be difficult to measure, too. Crase et al.'s work on consultation on the Murray-Darling Basin suggests the importance of understanding the structure of the problem that the consultation is meant to affect. Cost–benefit analysis, sensitively carried out, can often expose poor priority setting *ex ante* (Crase et al. 2005). By seeing costs and benefits from the community's and government's perspectives, this kind of analysis (even if quantitative data are limited) forces those organising consultation to see the issues as a whole.

We could not get political 'buy-in'

The Netherlands has experimented with a number of interactive processes for civic redesign, which attempt to involve citizens in decision making. One of the problems of these processes is the tendency for the consultation and the politics to remain separate—a version of the 'multiple streams' described in Chapter 4. Together with two colleagues, the Dutch academic Juriaan Edelenbos undertook a comparative study of interactive processes for urban redesign in five Dutch municipalities: De Bilt, Hellevoetsluis, Leerdam, Zeewolde and Enschede (Mayer et al. 2005). Process-based evaluative criteria of accountability, learning and cooperation were chosen for the study.

One key type of cooperation identified in the empirical work was that between elected officials, civil servants and citizens' groups. As summarised in an overview published in 2005, in only one of the municipalities (Leerdam) was there sufficient cooperation to ensure continuing political ownership of the preferences voiced through the consultation process. In the others (of which Enschede was the example), the necessary cooperation could not be achieved.

Enschede is a city of 150 000 people, with a historic town centre, the Stadcerf. The mayor of the city proposed a project to rejuvenate the city, with improved pedestrian access and major renovations of buildings and streetscapes. The process involved three key groups: a reference group consisting of civil servants, a group of businesspeople and a consultative group consisting of representatives from citizens' interest groups. Unfortunately, the businesspeople (who had the financial power) tended to bypass the consultative process and talked directly to the council officials. For their part, the council officials had little contact with the citizens' groups.

How could the process have been better managed?

For the Dutch researchers, this experience suggested the importance of avoiding 'parallel trajectories'—that is, an interactive process with few connections to the 'real' process. Remedies included:

- the involvement of political office-holders from the earliest stages
- provision for feedback between interactive and conventional processes.

The Dutch researchers concluded that political executives needed to be 'brought along' with the interactive process to minimise the possibility that they would reject outcomes that could be awkward or bothersome (Edelenbos 2005).

Summing up

Many engagement problems derive from a failure (by public managers and other professionals) to consider the process from the point of view of those being consulted. Mistakes can be avoided by constructing what is familiar (to the public manager) as unfamiliar (that is, requiring explanation). Even seemingly intractable problems, such as bureaucratic silos, can be overcome when there is a will to do so. Elaborate forms of inter-agency coordination might not be necessary. With support from agency leaders, it is possible for managers on the ground to overcome many of the bureaucratic sins of consultation by discovering and using flexible ways of working within the one agency.

Responding to the political dimensions of consultation requires an acute appreciation of context. In Australian government, achieving political buy-in is often difficult because public servants are in the position of reacting to decisions already made (or being made) at the political level. In these situations, in which the politics of conflict are involved, distinguishing negotiation from consultation becomes important. Trying to do deals through consultative processes is almost certainly to overload them.

Endnotes

[1] Llewellyn Reinders, speaking at Dilemmas of Engagement Forum, 22 August 2008.

[2] The *Swedish Group Proceedings Act*, which came into force in January 2003, makes it possible for the Environmental Protection Agency to use the Environment Court to seek environmental injunctions or damages on behalf of a group of citizens (see <www.eu2006.bmsg.gv.at/cms/eu2006/attachments/4/2/7/CH0604/CMS1133429025309/renfors.pdf>).

[3] This case study comes from Durey and Lockhart (2004).

6. Risks, opportunities and challenges

Where to next? There are, evidently, many engagement contexts in which practice has evolved and consolidated over time and policy makers are comfortable using fairly standardised techniques. As for innovation, there is no one 'cutting edge', but a number of possibilities for further development.

People are experimenting with numerous new modalities, particularly in relation to deliberation—that is, where engagement does not aim simply to elicit what is already there, but to actively involve citizens and groups in discussion and change. For public managers, there are many options to be tested. Equally, however, there are problems in reconciling the world of collective decision making with the world of engagement. Issues of power and control, risk and challenge—the dilemmas of engagement—need to be teased out.

As with many innovative processes in governance, going further requires a good understanding of the risks involved. The case studies assembled for this volume, as well as others from the literature, suggest three types, or dimensions, of risk:

- risks relating to context
- risks relating to motivation
- risks relating to operations.

Understanding context

We have seen that, overwhelmingly, the specifics of the situation define the parameters of engagement. For most public servants, most of the time, the menu of choice is restricted by the requirements of the job to be done. A particular outcome is required—such as a usable piece of legislation or delivery of a program to a particular group—and engagement flows from that.

So, context shapes engagement. What, however, determines context? Clearly, the level of government is important, as is the history of governance in the particular area under consideration. Whether we 'consult'—that is, gauge reactions or opinions—or engage participants more directly depends largely on the nature of the situation. In theory, consultation is the 'freest' mode because it can be undertaken wherever consultees can be identified. By contrast, participation, in any meaningful sense, cannot simply be conjured out of thin air.

In general, though, participatory processes are less risky than consultative ones. This might seem counter-intuitive until we remember the key importance of context. Participation will not be on the menu of choices unless there has been some progress made towards governance. Participatory decision making in natural resource management demonstrated the importance of evolved governance together with clear warrants for action. Our case studies show what can be accomplished in these settings—for example, in the use of participatory decision making to resolve conflicts over access to resources in the tuna fisheries off the eastern and western Australian coasts.

Consultation, on the other hand, often takes place in situations of high conflict, high ambiguity and uncertain or wavering political support. These problems can be particularly acute at state and territory levels. Issues requiring consultation are those that affect significant groups, as well as those that affect the natural environment and/or citizens' rights and entitlements. These are also areas where risk is likely to be highest (Government of the ACT 2004).

Equally, however, there are risks in not consulting in these situations. Decisions might be wrong (because of a lack of information) or they might have little support from affected groups (for a variety of reasons). Potential political penalties should be considered as a major factor. Politicians and their advisers want public servants to alert them to danger. They do not want to be caught out by unexpected opposition.

What's your motivation?

Consultation manuals stress being clear about the purpose of the consultation: what might (or might not) happen as a result of it. This view of purpose relates to the content of consultation—the policy, practice or decision that is its object. Beyond these purposes, however, lies the Realpolitik of motivation. What does the government hope to gain? Is it support? The neutralising of opposition? None of the above?

The will to consult does not always translate into the will to make policy change. Reviews are frequently used to defuse opposition and to disarm alternative views, rather than to deal with them. Some issues, such as innovation policy, are visited and revisited over the years, without ever penetrating the policy agenda. Recommendations are made—for example, to deal with a lack of commercialisation of Australian research and development—without action being taken.

Using consultation in this way—that is, to rationalise inaction—can be frustrating for those involved, but it is relatively low risk. Using consultation to claim legitimacy for a decision that has already been taken is a higher-risk strategy, because disappointed communities are likely to express their dismay politically. In these cases, consultation can damage trust, rather than helping to build it up.

Public servants are right to be wary of consultation when issues are too 'raw' or when value conflict is high. In these instances, governments prefer to distance themselves from the arena, by using royal commissions or creating special commissions of inquiry. A prominent figure is appointed to head the inquiry, with public servants providing secretariat and back-up resources. Even so, the result can be predetermined. More often than not, values or guiding orientations are either assumed or are inserted politically.

In other situations, governments are often not quite sure what they want to achieve when they consult. As we know, when the objective is unclear, it is difficult to find the 'right' technique. There is often a trade-off between blandness and engagement. Information can be gathered without arousing alarm if the questions are sufficiently innocuous. A planning 'strategy' for part of a town or city might elicit few responses. When it comes to abrupt changes to cherished neighbourhoods, the result might be quite different.

It could be argued that a sense of the Realpolitik of engagement is inherent in the arts of bureaucratic and political judgment. As the demand for engagement grows, however, so does the need for more explicit risk assessment. The strategic motivation for the engagement should be carefully thought through.

Operational risks

Context and motivation shape the parameters of risk, so understanding these factors is clearly crucial. There are, however, also operational risks that should be identified and dealt with. These risks derive largely from flows of information that might not be understood or anticipated.

Clearly, consultation is meant to improve information flow, but there are dangers in becoming 'captive' to information from some consultees, particularly those with political power. As a seasoned regulator put it, 'You make sure you have input from all the players. If you don't get them, you go and find them. They themselves are the checks and balances that prevent capture.' [1]

What happens when there is a parallel process—that is, interests are lobbying ministers and advisers as well as taking part in consultations? Experienced managers stress that it all depends on whether you can find out what is going on or not. Acquiring this intelligence depends on developing and maintaining good relationships with ministers' offices. If this is not possible, the best safeguard is your professionalism in what you are doing.

How to reduce the risk of disappointed or angered consultees wreaking vengeance on the government? Two of the few saving graces in these situations are transparency and fairness. Sometimes, being prepared to take the public into one's confidence might be the best form of risk management. Being prepared to listen is of key importance here. As one consultee put it, 'I did not like the outcome, but at least I felt I had been heard. [2] '

Engagement and program implementation

Perhaps because of the influence of policy cycles, there is a tendency to think of engagement as taking place when policy is being formulated, well before the phase of 'implementation'. From a public management point of view, however, the real opportunities and rewards might lie after implementation. Making decisions about difficult issues is a job for politicians. Implementation, on the other hand, is acknowledged as the domain of public managers, and public servants, not politicians, are blamed when it goes wrong.

Despite a large academic literature on implementation, there is little agreement about the nature of the processes involved. I want to suggest that there is much to be gained by seeing implementation from an 'engagement' point of view. There are certainly some leads in this direction that might be taken from the literature. Indeed, Nakamura and Smallwood stress communication as being the pre-eminent implementation activity. By communication, they do not simply mean deliberation, but the activities through which policy choices—such as a new program or a change in regulation—are turned into organisational actions (Nakamura and Smallwood 1980).

Traditionally, agencies implemented policy and programs through hierarchical forms of communication. With the advent of outsourcing and a greater emphasis on partnerships, this communication takes place within inter-organisational, rather than intra-organisational, contexts. Depending on the types of relationships that are involved, and the degree of cooperation required from partners, communication can involve consultative elements. Collaboration (combining with other agencies or groups to achieve jointly defined purposes) and co-production (producing outputs with the involvement of other agencies or groups) each imply spaces, opportunities and, on occasion, requirements for consultation. It is not just service delivery that is involved. We saw that the ACCC, a statutory body in the regulatory field, consulted extensively in the implementation of its work.

It is true that the relationships involved in partnering have been extensively studied; however, the communicative dimensions of these relationships, and their practical implications, remain relatively unremarked. There are many issues here—for example, how can the distinctive attributes of partnering be retained, while conforming to public sector criteria relating to due process, reporting and planning? Can partners in delivery also be partners in policy? How should partners be consulted when issues to do with the overall purpose and configuration of relationships are under discussion? The dilemma here is how best to reconcile the needs of government with those of governance. As an experienced community worker put it, 'Consultation often tries to be cooptation. Governments talk about collaboration when they mean coordination.' [3] Coordination, however, as an activity of power that allocates priorities, cannot readily be reconciled with the give and take of genuine collaboration.

Networking

Successful public managers are good networkers, in the sense that they can bring circles of influence to bear on particular problems. We saw evidence of these networks in policymaking situations, but they were less apparent when it came to implementation. As formal implementing mechanisms, networks in Australia are less developed than in other jurisdictions—for example, regional development networks in some of the states of the United States, social inclusion networks in the United Kingdom and planning networks in the Netherlands. The Australian Job Network contains many 'co-production' relationships, but offers few opportunities for cross-organisational networking. [4]

As 'silo-busting' mechanisms, networks tend to fail because they lack incentives for the participants to continue to exchange information (see Keast and Brown 2006). Outputs/outcomes budgeting and reporting can make these problems worse, because of measurement difficulties. The return of forms of evaluation that recognise cross-portfolio contributions can provide a way forward here, but equally, senior managers should recognise networking as a form of communication within an overall context of engagement.

Collaboration

Collaborative arrangements involve entities working together to achieve mutually agreed goals. From a public sector point of view, collaborations commonly involve other agencies, NGOs and, on occasion, business. Collaboration is also a type of engagement or, to put the matter around the other way, engagement techniques are required for successful collaboration. There are many examples of successful collaborations in which participants have complementary skills—for example, research collaborations and collaborations to achieve health outcomes. There could, in the future, be collaborations designed to achieve greenhouse-gas reductions, in the sense of facilitating information exchange.

The maintenance of collaborative relationships depends on shared understandings and values. For these reasons, they require longer-term commitment than do networks (see Head 2007). Such concord can be difficult to achieve when the participants are very diverse and when the funding, as it often does, emanates mostly from government. In funding NGOs, governments might not be looking for collaboration as an outcome—they want other benefits: access to the speed of the NGO, its dedicated workforce, and so on. Identifying and acting on these value conflicts can be the key to unlocking the potential of these forms.

Co-production

Co-production is more than contracting. It refers to modes of joint governance between government and the private (usually not-for-profit) sector, particularly in fields such as child care, care of the elderly and, increasingly, education. Good contract managers know the value of talking with providers 'around' as well as 'about' the contractual relationship.

There is, however, a need, and an opportunity, for broader consultative arrangements involving contractors. The 'feedback' loop to policy making can be poorly articulated when delivery, implementation and policy advice are separated. Arguably, when information is disrupted in this way, the need for consultation increases proportionately. Oddly though, in practice, consultation for co-production can be poorly developed. Contractors—particularly those outside the community sector—might not be admitted to the inner circle of policy making: they are regarded simply as hired guns. For their part, agencies are required to maintain a level playing field between providers and to conduct 'open' conversations about tenders.

Formal compacts are one way of reducing misunderstanding. Through compacts, some governments have shown that they are sensitive to the need not to use their market power as buyers and as contract managers to silence the advocacy role of partner organisations. Undertakings to consult in relation to bureaucratic decision making might also be in order here. It might, however, be equally productive for contract managers to get 'out and about' a bit more, to exploit the opportunities for consultation and feedback that can be experienced only in less formal contexts.

Challenges

As we have seen, there are many opportunities for the development of engagement practice. Identifying these opportunities comes as much from seeing existing processes and structures in new ways and developing potential that is already there as it does from trying new forms. There are, however, a number of fundamental challenges to be surmounted—and dilemmas to be addressed—before opportunities can be embraced.

Flexibility

One of the abiding problems of government is getting departments and agencies to work together. Much has been written on the subject, and the Commonwealth Government's Management Advisory Committee (MAC) has produced one of the definitive practitioner-oriented documents on the subject, *Connecting Government* (MAC 2004).

The term 'whole of government' has been used to describe the problem and the solution. 'Whole of government' can, however, be more hindrance than help in coming up with answers. The dilemmas of engagement suggest that the challenge is, rather, one of overcoming the disincentives that prevent sensible communication.

When a public servant from one department rings another seeking information, the immediate response is to find reasons for not giving it. Stances in IDCs are often competitive, rather than cooperative. Competition, however, tends to dry up flows of information. Collegiality should be a 'spirit for all occasions', not just when crisis strikes (Shergold 2007).

The growing importance of minister's offices—and of networks operating from the Prime Minister's office—might be as much a reaction against over-zealous bureaucratic politics as a result of overweening adviser power. There is certainly evidence that former Prime Minister John Howard, when he wanted change, would bypass conventional ways of working—for example, by using task forces that brought those who were normally outside government into the heart of the decision-making process (Stewart and Maley 2007).

It would be wrong, however, to assume that blockages to information flow occur predominantly at the most senior levels. We know, for example, that departmental secretaries are in regular contact with each other, in formal and informal ways. The problem of inadequate information flow might be more apparent in the middle of agencies—where power might be perceived as deriving from withholding information—rather than at the bottom or the top.

How to counter this kind of defensiveness? Our case studies suggested the importance of senior-level support and flexibility. Giving additional flexibility at the lower levels might not be as difficult as some might think. For these boundary riders, communication becomes a raison d'être. Agencies must, however, be prepared to allow information to flow more freely in order to make this happen—to empower people to make decisions about what to say and what to withhold and to trust them (with appropriate training) to make the right choices.

Inclusion

Consultative forums offer opportunities for floating new ideas. Program evaluations provide a broad canvas for listening and observing. There is, however, more room for free-flowing forms of discussion that bring together participants who do not normally talk to each other. Such innovative forums might fail, but they might also be a much-needed source of good ideas and practical steps towards change.

There are signs that agencies are at least thinking about how to open up communication pathways in order to more effectively engage the community. An AusAID study commissioned in the context of the 2006 *White Paper on Australian Aid* stressed the importance of bringing researchers, public servants, NGOs and development contractors together in ways that bypassed the expected channels of communication and the relationships they implied (Hart and Shipley 2005:6).

Inviting 'in' those who are normally left out can be the most exciting challenge of all. The mentally ill, drug users, homeless people and disadvantaged communities exhaust the patience of many helpers. Using engagement in ways that help to empower communities is often a last resort. The rewards here, however, can be much greater than the risks.

Language

Engagement is about communication and communication is about language. There is, however, a language of engagement that might itself be impeding progress. The consultation forum convened for this research returned a number of times to this theme. As one expert expressed it: 'Language can be a real blocker. Words like "partnership" need to be replaced by something else—"reciprocity", for example. Words like "consultation" and even "participation" imply processes that people may (or may not) be invited into.'[5]

Governments can be too focused, too binary in their thinking. As one seasoned cross-bench politician put it, 'There are two kinds of consultation: when governments want to know, and when governments want to tell.' Often, however, this kind of determination to structure the communication in a particular way sells the process short. 'Governments should try to understand, not persuade or decide.'

Traditional forms of engagement revolve around official types of language. The community is 'invited' to put in a submission. Once the terminology becomes set, there is a risk that it precludes the fluidity that should result from these relationships. Or alternatively, relationships can be construed in very prosaic terms, without any sense of the reciprocity they should imply. Most of those delivering services under contract, for example, do not believe they are engaged in 'co-production', still less collaboration.

The challenge of language is about flexibility and having the willingness to listen. It also comes down to having more time. Public servants (and professionals generally) have too few opportunities to simply 'chew the fat', or even to get out and about without having a key performance indicator hanging around their necks. They need more time—to experience, to savour and to learn.

Settings

Suggesting, as I have, that more time is needed for policy making is all very well. Ultimately, however, public policy is about making choices. Deliberation might be extensive, even around the cabinet table, but at some point, a preference for one option rather than another must be determined. The necessity to make a decision does not always fit with the time (or the timing) that is most conducive to the kinds of information that are furnished by engagement.

There might be a pre-election rush or events suddenly bring to the fore an issue that has been quietly simmering away on the backburners of government. There is simply no time to engage in a systematic way. Nevertheless, the effectiveness of the choice will depend on the information on which it is based and decision makers must rely on the quality control of their advisers in this respect.

Politics necessarily reigns in these situations. These circumstances, however, also highlight the value of informal consultative networks resting on more formal structures—such as consultative committees. In addition, the opportunities created by implementation-related consultation—provided they are recognised as such—can give the confidence that is needed to respond quickly.

Control

From the Public Service perspective, consultation must be carefully managed, so that governments do not cede control over processes for which they are accountable. Formal accountability works vertically: up to the minister and from the minister to the Parliament. Public managers are wary of processes that might lead to a loss of control.

Collaboration, in particular, poses problems of accountability, because standard accountability arrangements depend on a specified agency spending appropriated funds to achieve an agreed output (or objective). The Australian National Audit Office (ANAO 2007) cautions that alternative arrangements should be established only when the complexity of the situation warrants it. Moreover, there should be a lead agency, so that accountabilities are clear.

A number of possibilities suggest themselves as answers to this challenge. Flexibility within participatory contexts—without the need for formal machinery—has already been mentioned. Trust—where it can be engendered and sustained—is crucial in overcoming communication deficits. More radically, encouraging a measure of accountability to communities—as well as of communities to government—might be the only way of overcoming the top-down bias of centralised governance. If these processes empower communities, that might be the best result of all.

Summing up

The rewards of engagement are enhanced legitimacy and better information. The risks lie in capture, backlash and confused accountabilities. Managing these risks means having a good strategic perspective—that is, an overview of the costs and benefits of different courses of action and an understanding of the Realpolitik (knowing the stakes for politicians, agencies and communities).

At the same time, there are opportunities for the development of engagement in areas of lower risk, notably in relation to the implementation of policy. Implementation is traditionally the domain of public managers, and the continuing use of contracted service providers gives space and opportunity not just for negotiation in individual instances, but for continuing interaction at the policymaking level—that is, where the policy of implementation is under discussion.

The principal challenge for public servants in charting a forward course is to balance formal and informal ways of communicating with stakeholders. The protocols of accountability and control prescribe formal conversations: where what is said, and to whom, are on the public record. On the other hand, public business would grind to a halt without the informal conversations that establish context and hopefully clarify intentions. Effective engagement seems to require the experience, judgment and confidence to know which modality is appropriate and when to make the switch.

Endnotes

[1] Consultation forum, University of Canberra, 22 August 2008.

[2] Consultation forum, University of Canberra, 22 August 2008.

[3] Consultation forum, University of Canberra, 22 August 2008.

[4] The Howard Government established the Job Network in 1998. It is a national network of not-for-profit and for-profit agencies, which compete for contracts to deliver services to unemployed people, including training and job placements.

[5] Barbara Pamphilon, Consultation Forum, 22 August 2008.

Conclusion

As we look towards the future of engagement, can we say that more participation is likely to work better than less? The answer depends, in large part, on whether participants in general, and governments in particular, are able to overcome a number of fundamental constraints. On the one hand, governments need the kinds of information that engagement provides. On the other, obtaining this information is neither cost free nor without risk.

There are a number of tensions, or dilemmas, at the heart of engagement. There is a tension between the Realpolitik of power and the need to keep faith with communities. There is a tension between the need to maintain control and the need for flexibility. There is a tension between the precision of official language and custom and the need to talk to communities in ways that they understand.

The more important it is for governments to engage—in the sense that the issues involved are likely to be of concern to citizens—the less likely it is that they will do so. Worried about the risks involved, governments either consult blandly or consult in bad faith. They believe that conflict is to be avoided at all costs. At the same time, if governments are doing their job properly, they will necessarily make decisions that offend sections of the community. If consultation is to be judged according to the extent to which it creates consensus, it is clearly doomed.

How, then, should these widely varying processes and practices be judged? And how should public managers evaluate the costs and benefits involved? If public managers are to apply a public interest test, they should be satisfied with their achievements only when the forms of engagement that they sponsor really make a difference, which raises a further question: 'difference to whom?' In the case of participatory governance, the answer is clearly 'difference to the participants' (remembering that in this sense, government is also a participant). Participatory governance, to be judged successful, must be reaching places and cases that more traditional administrative forms cannot.

For consultation, it might be that we should be asking not 'what difference did it make?' but 'was the process successful?'. In other words, did those taking part in the process view it favourably? I have suggested that there are steps agencies can take to lessen the risk that the process will leave participants feeling let down. Agencies' needs and citizens' expectations can be quite different. If, however, there is clear thinking on the part of agencies about their motivation, it is less likely that they will encourage false expectations among citizens.

Beyond the practical, there are normative questions about governance that need to be considered. To what extent should those who are hard to reach be consulted? Those possessing structural power do not, as a rule, need to be invited in. Those who do not possess this power do need to be invited in; the question is, invited in to what and to what effect? Ultimately, policy processes that impinge on the powerful must be participatory, in the sense that what happens in reality, as distinct from what is in the legislation, will reflect their capacity, if they wish to do so, to evade or to bend the rules. Those with less ability to exercise influence might simply slip through the cracks, their voices unheard.

For public managers wishing to expand the boundaries of engagement, there is some room to exercise values leadership in this direction, but norms must always be served by practicalities. The evidence suggests that those who are hard to reach might be better served by smaller-scale, more participatory forms of governance than by more diffuse, deliberative exercises.

Given the practical importance of context, and the imperatives of politics, it is unclear how much discretion there is for public servants to choose between what are, in effect, differing consultative designs. Capacity, and the self-concept of the Public Service, will be important in creating the confidence to make these judgments in ways that enhance the scope for consultation. A public service that is able to play multiple roles will have more room to experiment and to innovate than one that is trapped by convention. The political executive, and the middle and senior levels of the Public Service, should be prepared to allow this freedom.

A theoretical point is important here. It is unfortunate that information giving is always assigned to the lowest level of the consultation ladder. If governments are always on 'transmit' and never on 'receive', such an assignment is understandable. Two-way information-flow, however, in whatever context it takes place, is the essence, the fundamental raison d'être, of all forms of engagement.

If we regard policy making as a form of iterative communication, information exchange—using that term to mean communication of ideas, interests and needs—becomes its most characteristic activity. It follows from this that if there is one organisational change that agencies need to make in order to foster engagement, it is to think more creatively about how they communicate with the outside world.

Bibliography

Australian National Audit Office (ANAO) 2007, *Audit Focus*, August 2007, viewed 22 October 2008, www.anao.gov.au/

Arnstein, S. 1969 'A ladder of citizen participation', Journal of the American Planning Association, vol. 35, no. 4, pp 216-224.

Bachrach, P. and Baratz, M. S. 1962, 'The two faces of power', *American Political Review*, vol. 56, pp. 947–52.

Benkler, Y. 2006, *The Wealth of Networks: How social production transforms markets and freedom*, Yale University Press, New Haven.

Bishop, P. and Davis, G. 2002, 'Mapping public participation in policy choices', *Australian Journal of Public Administration*, vol. 61, no. 1, pp. 14–29.

Booher, D. and Innes, J. 2002, 'Network power in collaborative planning', *Journal of Planning Education and Research*, vol. 21, no. 3, pp. 221–36.

Cameron, J. and Grant-Smith, D. 2005, 'Building citizens: participatory planning practice and a transformative politics of difference', *Urban Policy and Research*, vol. 23, no. 1, pp. 21–36.

Carruthers, R., Latcham, B. and Pudney, S. 2006, *Volumetric Conversion in SE South Australia—Changing perceptions, mindsets and knowledge barriers before changing water licences*, Australasia Pacific Extension Network, viewed 9 November 2008, http://www.regional.org.au

Carson, L. 2006, *An Inventory of Democratic Deliberative Processes in Australia: Early findings*, viewed 4 November 2008, http://activedemocracy.net/articles

Carson, L., Sargant, C. and Blackadder, J. 2004, *Consult Your Community: A guide to running a youth jury*, NSW Premier's Department, Sydney, viewed 4 November 2008, http://activedemocracy.net/parrayouth

Catt, H. and Murphy, M. 2003, 'What voice for the people? Categorising methods of public consultation', *Australian Journal of Political Science*, vol. 38, no. 3, pp. 407–21.

Chen, P. 2004 'A comparative analysis of political email lists', Paper presented to the Australian Electronic Governance Conference 2004, viewed 12 April 2009, http://www.public-policy.unimelb.edu.au/egovernance/ConferenceContent.html.

Chen, P. 2007, *Electronic Engagement: A guide for public sector managers*, ANU E Press, Canberra.

Colebatch, H. 2002 *Policy* (2nd edition), Open University Press, Buckingham.

Commonwealth of Australia 2003, *Review of the Corporate Governance of Statutory Authorities and Office Holders*, [*Uhrig Report*], Canberra, viewed 4 November 2008, www.finance.gov.au

Crase, L., Dollery, B. and Wallis, J. 2005, 'Community consultation in public policy: the case of the Murray-Darling Basin of Australia', *Australian Journal of Political Science*, vol. 40, no. 2, pp. 221–37.

Department of Health and Ageing 1995, *Ways Forward: National Aboriginal and Torres Strait Islander mental health policy national consultancy report*, viewed 6 May 2008, http://www.health.gov.au/internet/main/publishing.nsf

Dryzek, J. 1990, *Discursive Democracy: Politics, policy and political science*, Cambridge University Press, New York.

Dryzek, J. 2000, *Deliberative Democracy and Beyond: Liberals, critics, contestations*, Oxford University Press, Oxford.

Dugdale, A. 2008, 'New arenas for public life: negotiating health on-line', *Australian Journal of Political Science*, vol. 43, no. 1, pp. 27–41.

Durey, A. and Lockhart, C. 2004, 'A review of community consultation in the development of a multi-purpose service in rural and remote Australia', *Australian Health Review*, vol. 28, no. 1, pp. 97–104.

Edelenbos, J. 1999, 'Design and management of participatory public policy making', *Public Management*, vol. 1, no. 4, pp. 568–78.

Edelenbos, J. 2005, 'Institutional implications of interactive governance: insights from Dutch practice', *Governance*, vol. 18, no. 1, pp. 111–34.

Edwards, M. 2008, *Participatory Governance*, University of Canberra, Canberra.

Environment Protection Authority of New South Wales 1998, *A Review of Community Consultation*, Environment Protection Authority of New South Wales, viewed 3 November 2008, http://www.environment.nsw.gov.au

Fishkin, J. 2003, 'Consulting the public through deliberative polling', *Journal of Policy Analysis and Management*, vol. 22, no. 1, pp. 128–33.

Fung, Archon 2006, 'Democratizing the policy process', in M. Moran, M. Rein and R. E. Goodin (eds), *Oxford Handbook of Public Policy*, Oxford University Press, New York, pp. 669–88.

Fung, Archon 2007, 'Democratic theory and political science: a pragmatic method of constructive engagement', *American Political Science Review*, vol. 101, no. 3, pp. 443–58.

Goodin, R. 2003, *Reflective Democracy*, Oxford University Press.

Government of the Australian Capital Territory (Government of the ACT) 2004, *The Social Compact: A partnership between the community sector and the ACT Government*, Government of the Australian Capital Territory, Canberra, viewed 10 November 2008, http:// www.act.gov.au

Government of Western Australia n.d., *Community Consultation Document for the Draft Water Quality Improvement Plan for the Rivers and Estuary of the Peel-Harvey System*, Environmental Protection Authority, www.epa.wa.gov.au

Government of Western Australia 2008, *Welcome to Network City*, Department for Planning and Infrastructure, viewed 19 October 2008, www.dpi.wa.gov.au

Grant, R. 2005, *The Uhrig review and the future of statutory authorities*, Parliamentary Library Research Note, no. 50, 2004–05, viewed 4 November 2008, www.aph.gov.au/library

Hart, G. and Shipley, E. 2005, *Engaging the Australian Community: Analytical report for the White Paper on Australia's aid program*, AusAID, Canberra, viewed 2 November 2008, www.ausaid.gov.au/publications/whitepaper

Head, B. 2007, 'Community engagement: participation on whose terms?', *Australian Journal of Political Science*, vol. 42, no. 3, pp. 441–54.

Head, B. and Stewart, J. 2007, Evaluating policy processes, Paper presented to the conference Governing by Looking Back: How history matters in society, Research School of Social Sciences, The Australian National University, 12–14 December 2007.

Hendriks, C. 2002, 'Institutions of deliberative democratic processes and interest groups: roles, tensions and incentives', *Australian Journal of Public Administration*, vol. 61, no. 1, pp. 64–75.

Hill, R. and Roughley, L. 1997, 'Public consultation and juvenile justice reform: a Queensland case study', *Australian Journal of Social Issues*, vol. 32, no. 1, pp. 21–36.

Holland, I. 2002, 'Consultation, constraints and norms: the case of nuclear waste', *Australian Journal of Public Administration*, vol. 61, no. 1, pp. 76–86.

Inner Sydney Regional Council for Social Development Inc. 2008, *Inner Sydney Voice*, issue 111, Spring.

Irvine, R. and Stansbury, J. 2004, 'Citizen participation in decision making: is it worth the effort?', *Public Administration Review*, vol. 64, no. 1, pp. 55–65.

Jarvie, W. 2008, 'Working differently to make a difference in indigenous communities', *Public Administration Today*, January–March, pp. 5–13.

Jeffries, S. 2008, Address to the National Institute of Governance, University of Canberra, 18 September 2008, Paper presented at the Australian Electronic Governance Conference 2004, viewed 15 November 2008, http://www.public-policy.unimelb.edu.au/egovernance/ConferenceContent.html

Joseph, R. 2004, The limits of electronic government: the value of an information perspective, Paper presented at the Australian Electronic Governance Conference 2004, viewed 15 November 2008, http://www.public-policy.unimelb.edu.au/egovernance/ConferenceContent.html

Keast, R. and Brown, K. 2006, 'Adjusting to new ways of working: experiments with service delivery in the public sector', *Australian Journal of Public Administration*, vol. 65, no. 4, pp. 41–53.

Kickert, J., Klijn, E. and Koppenjaan, J. 1997, *Managing Complex Networks: Strategies for the public sector*, Sage, London.

Lukensmeyer, C. and Torres, L. 2006, *Public Deliberation: A manager's guide to citizen engagement*, IBM Centre for the Business of Government, http://www.businessofgovernment.org/main/publications/grant_reports/details/index.asp?GID=239

Management Advisory Committee (MAC) 2004, *Connecting Government: Whole of government responses to Australia's priority challenges*, Australian Public Service Commission, Canberra, www.apsc.gov.au/mac

March, J. 1989, *Rediscovering Institutions: The organisational basis of politics*, Free Press, New York.

Marsh, I. 2002, 'Governance in Australia: emerging issues and achievements', *Australian Journal of Public Administration*, vol. 61, no. 2, pp. 3–9.

Mayer, I., Edelenbos, J. and Monnikhof, R. 2005, 'Interactive policy development: undermining or sustaining democracy', *Public Administration*, vol. 83, no. 1, pp. 179–99.

Mercer, D. 2000, *A Question of Balance: Natural resource conflict issues in Australia*, Third edition, Federation Press, Sydney.

Nakamura, R. and Smallwood, F. 1980, *The Politics of Policy Implementation*, St Martin's Press, New York.

NSW 2006 *NSW Implementation Plan for the National Water Initiative*, viewed 12 April 2009, http:// www.nwc.gov.au/resources/documents .

Oakley, S. 2007, 'Public consultation and place-marketing in the revitalisation of the Port Adelaide waterfront', *Urban Policy and Research*, vol. 25, no. 1, pp. 113–28.

OATSIH 1994, *National Aboriginal Health Strategy: An evaluation*, Department of Health and Ageing, Canberra, viewed 4 November 2008, http://www.health.gov.au

Organisation for Economic Cooperation and Development (OECD), 2001, *Citizens As Partners*, Organisation for Economic Cooperation and Development, Paris.

Organisation for Economic Cooperation and Development (OECD) 2003, *Open Government: Fostering dialogue with civil society*, Organisation for Economic Cooperation and Development, Paris.

Parker, J. 2008, 'Leichhardt Mayor, Jamie Parker—victory for community on Callan Park', Friends of Callan Park Blog Archive, viewed 9 November 2008, http://www.callanpark.com/?p=191

Pateman, C. 1970, *Participation and Democratic Theory*, Cambridge University Press, Cambridge.

Prasser, S. 2006, *Royal Commissions and Public Inquiries in Australia*, LexisNexis.

Prasser, S. 2007, 'Queensland's burning—local government amalgamations Beattie-style', *On Line Opinion*, 27 September, viewed 10 November 2008, http://www.onlineopinion.com.au

Pross, P. 1986, *Group Politics and Public Policy*, Oxford University Press, Toronto.

Rawls, J. 1997, 'The idea of public reason revisited', *The University of Chicago Law Review*, vol. 64, no. 3, Summer, pp. 765–807.

Reddel, T. and Woolcock, G. 2004, 'From consultation to participatory governance? A critical review of citizen engagement strategies in Queensland', *Australian Journal of Public Administration*, vol. 63, no. 3, pp. 75–85.

Rogers, C. 2006, *Palerang Council Visioning Workshops*, Summary Report, Palerang Council, viewed 4 November 2008, www.tallaganda.nsw.gov.au

Ryan, N. 1995, 'Ministerial advisers', in Jenny Stewart (ed.), *From Hawke to Keating: Australian Commonwealth Administration 1990–93*, University of Canberra and Royal Institute of Public Administration Australia.

Sabatier, P. (ed.) 1999, *Theories of the Policy Process*, Westview Press, Boulder, Colo.

Sawer, M. 2002, 'Governing for the mainstream: implications for community representation', *Australian Journal of Public Administration*, vol. 61, no. 1, pp. 39–49.

Senate Standing Committee on Rural and Regional Affairs and Transport 2007, *Options for Additional Water Supplies for South East Queensland*, The Senate, Canberra, www.aph.gov.au/Senate

Sharman, C. 2006, Citizens' assemblies and parliamentary reform in Canada, Senate Occasional Lecture Series, 31 March 2006, viewed 2 November 2008, www.aph.gov.au/Senate

Shergold, P. 2005, 'Coping with crisis: personal reflections on what the public service learned from the tsunami disaster', *Public Administration Today*, October–December, pp. 43–8.

Shergold, P. 2007, 'The 30th anniversary: future challenges for administrative review', *Administrative Review*, vol. 58, pp. 20–6.

Snowden, D. and Boone, M. 2007, 'A leader's framework in decision making', *Harvard Business Review*, November.

Stanhope, J. 2008, Community central in major consultation reform, viewed 6 October 2008, http://www.chiefminister.act.gov.au

Stewart, J. 2006, 'Value conflict and policy change', *Review of Policy Research*, vol. 23, no. 1, pp. 183–96.

Stewart, J. 2008a, *Public service independence and responsiveness: striking a balance*, Occasional Paper 2/2008, Academy of the Social Sciences in Australia, Canberra.

Stewart, J. 2008b, 'Saving the Mary River', *On Line Opinion*, 8 May 2008, viewed 10 November 2008, www.onlineopinion.com.au

Stewart, J. and Jones, G. 2003, *Renegotiating the Environment: The power of politics*, Sydney, Federation Press.

Stewart, J. and Maley, M. 2007, 'The Howard government and political management: the challenge of policy activism', *Australian Journal of Political Science*, June 2007, vol. 42, no. 2, pp. 277–94.

Success Works 2002, *Working Together: Integrated governance*, Success Works and Institute of Public Administration Australia.

Sullivan, H. and Skelcher, C. 2002, *Working Across Boundaries: Collaboration in public services*, Palgrave Macmillan, Basingstoke.

Sutcliffe, K. and Richardson, M. 2004, Remote area e-governance—the Gulf Savannah experience, Paper presented at the Australian Electronic Governance Conference 2004, viewed 15 November 2008, http://www.public-policy.unimelb.edu.au/egovernance/ConferenceContent.html

Sydney Harbour Foreshore Authority 2008, *Callan Park: Our places and projects*, viewed 9 November 2008, http://www.shfa.nsw.gov.au

Thacher, D. and Rein, M. 2004, 'Managing value conflict in public policy', *Governance*, vol. 17, no. 4, pp. 457–86.

Tiernan, A. 2007, *Power Without Responsibility*, UNSW Press, Sydney.

van de Meer, F.-B. and Edelenbos, J. 2006, 'Evaluation in multi-actor policy processes', *Evaluation*, vol. 12, no. 2, pp. 201–18.

Victorian Local Government Association (VLGA) n.d., *Best Value Victoria: Community consultation resource guide*, viewed 1 November 2008, www.vlga.org.au

Walters, L., Aydelotte, J. and Miller, J. 2000, 'Putting more public in policy analysis', *Public Administration Review*, vol. 60, no. 4, pp. 349–59.

Walters, M. 2005, 'Cops and consultation: police accountability teams in New South Wales', *Alternative Law Journal*, vol. 30, no. 3, pp. 112–15.

Weick, K. 2008, *People Whose Ideas Influence Organisational Work*, viewed 4 November 2008, www.onepine.info